MW01245397

Clean Your Inner House

A woman's journey to freedom and restoration

Mary Schulze Michener, Ed.D.

For God is not an indifferent bystander
(Heb. 12.28b).

Mobile, Alabama

ISBN 978-1-58169-474-1
For Worldwide Distribution
Printed in the U.S.A.

Gazelle Press
P.O. Box 191540 • Mobile, AL 36619
800-367-8203

This book is dedicated to my wonderful husband—
you have supported, encouraged, and loved me
unconditionally through this entire experience.
I wouldn't have been able to write this
without you.

Acknowledgments

Thank you to Chuck Ripka and Richard Sicheneder. Your friendship and ministry have allowed me to take a directive from God and see it through. You gave me the encouragement I needed to move away from fear.

To Kathy Weckwerth, you listened to God's nudge and invited me to be a part of Best Life Ministries. Sharing with women through this ministry has been an honor. In addition, your friendship has been life giving. Thank you.

To my family at Elk River UMC, you have loved, supported and encouraged me. You have let me practice delivering the message of this book in the pulpit and through Bible study. You are a gift to me and my family.

To my family, especially my sisters, you have been my cheerleaders every step of the way. You continually encourage me to press on even when the road is unclear. Thank you.

To my agent, Keith Carroll, I can't thank you enough for all your hard work. I kept asking God to bring me a publisher. He did one better—He brought you. Because you coached me through this process, the book is better. You did the work I didn't begin to know how to do so this book could go from dream to reality.

Thank you to everyone who encouraged me along the way. I took every word to heart and used it to keep going.

With joy and gratitude,
Mary Schulze Michener

Table of Contents

Preface

This all began on a leaders' retreat for our church. The morning opened with devotions on Matthew 26:39. Going a little farther, he fell with his face to the ground and prayed, "My Father, if it is possible, may this cup be taken from me. Yet not as I will, but as You will" (TNIV). Jesus surrendered His will to the will of His father. We were all encouraged to take our time of prayer and surrender ourselves to the will of God and press in on His will for us as a church. We spent the rest of the morning praying and seeking God's will.

Off I went. I often refer to my prayer time as schizophrenic. I needed to be moving, so I went on a walk with my journal, Bible, and iPod. Yes, my iPod. My worship playlist was on as I tried to clear my head and focus on God's will for our church.

As I walked, I saw lots of burnt trash that reminded me of our brokenness. Random thoughts ran through my head. Lead people to healing, marriage, abuse, wholeness. Then I prayed, "God give us the strength to be whole persons." Then I wrote this thought in my journal. "The more I am in right relationship with Him, the greater my sense of personal wholeness, and the greater my sense of His love and grace for me." Then I heard the song "Held," by Natalie Grant, playing on my iPod, and I began to cry. The lyrics reminded me of the hope we have in Him to heal our brokenness.

I asked God to give me a scripture. I heard Matthew 6:27 which says "Can any one of you by worrying add a single hour to your life?" (TNIV) I began laughing and said, "God you are funny! That's the first time You gave me a specific scripture to read and so appropriate." I think He was trying to tell me something.

What unfolded next has changed me profoundly. I asked God how we (the church) are supposed to do this (grow in ministry and expand the facility). God said very clearly, "Heal my people—write My book." I instantly knew what He meant. I was to start with

Him and tell my story of healing. Our dialogue continued in a way I had never experienced before.

Me: (Crying) "This is not what I expected."

God: "And that surprises you?"

Me: (Laughing again, I heard David Crowder's "No One Like You" on the iPod.) "Are You going to keep me focused?"

God: "You better believe it."

Me: "Do I have to tell it all?"

God: "Yes."

Me: "Even the deepest and the darkest?

God: "Yes, others need to know it is okay. That is the only way they are going to heal."

Me: (Crying again) "Why do you do this to me?"

God: "Because I love you."

Me: "It is so easy to not trust what I am hearing."

God: "Don't let him (evil one) get in the way."

Me: (Laughing and sarcastic) "This is supposed to be about bricks and mortar."

God: "It's never been about bricks and mortar."

Me: "Okay, I know, I know."

God: "Remember ERUMC meets all the needs of the community within and outside its walls. Ministry."

Me: "Oh, Lord, this is so big."

God: "Yep! That's why I am asking you."

Me: (Laughing and crying) "I don't know if I can take this."

God: "You'll be fine."

I then heard the song "Healing Rain."

Me: (Laughing) "You blow me away."

God: "Good."

Me: "I know we can do this."

God: "Yes, we can."

Me: "Do I read this to them (others on the retreat)?"
God: "Yes."
Me: "Why?"
God: "Accountability."
Me: "UGHHHHHH."

Finally, I heard the song "Worship You" and the lyrics, that say the best we can do is to worship Him. It was finally not about my kingdom but about His kingdom. This is not something I would have chosen to do on my own. I don't like writing. It's not my gifting. In fact, at first I didn't want to do any of this.

I had a lot of fear in the beginning. God, in His faithfulness, kept opening doors and putting people in my path to hold me up and show me His hand in this over and over. I wanted to fully trust Him and obey His call. All of this and knowing it was God's will that changed my heart, and I aligned my will with His. So I write this with joy while praying for His words to be written and for wholeness to be restored to all those who read this story.

Introduction

Welcome to my house. Would you like something to drink? Here, have a seat and relax for a while. I hope you find my house warm and inviting. There are no places you are not welcome. Every door has been opened. If you like, you can even look in my medicine cabinet and open my closet doors. I am not guaranteeing perfection. I am sure there is still some dust and disorganization. For the first time in my life, almost everything is where it belongs. God has been doing a lot of work to help me clean my house and now He wants me to invite you in to check it out. In Hebrews 12:25-27 (MSG) it states:

So don't turn a deaf ear to these gracious words. If those who ignored earthly warnings didn't get away with it, what will happen to us if we turn our backs on heavenly warnings? His voice that time shook the earth to its foundations; this time—he's told us this quite plainly—he'll also rock the heavens: "One last shaking, from top to bottom, stem to stern." The phrase "one last shaking" means a thorough housecleaning, getting rid of all the historical and religious junk so that the unshakable essentials stand clear and uncluttered.

So what does this scripture mean? God wants to clean our house, our emotional, spiritual house. It's His desire to set us free from the burdens life has given us. He wants us to be clean and uncluttered. "Why?" you ask. Who wouldn't do that for their children? As a parent, I would do anything to take away the suffering of my children. The cleaner we are, the better reflection of His love we can be to others.

And then in Hebrews 12:28-29, it says,

Do you see what we've got? An unshakable kingdom! And do you see how thankful we must be? Not only thankful, but brim-

ming with worship, deeply reverent before God. For God is not an indifferent bystander. He's actively cleaning house, torching all that needs to burn, and he won't quit until it's all cleansed. God himself is Fire!

Nothing could be truer; God is not a bystander. He will actively clean our hearts if we let Him. Sometimes His fire burns a little as He shows us the errors of our ways of thinking and understanding, but that is replaced with His love and comfort. In the end He restores us to a new creation. Of course this is a lifelong process. I'm still in the process. However, He sometimes chooses to clean big chunks at a time as He did with me. Once we enter into some housecleaning—maybe the closets or behind the fridge—we begin to see how great His love is for us. We have fewer burdens to clutter up our hearts so there is more room for Him.

I will share my story of emotional and spiritual healing from childhood sexual abuse. I will share the ups and downs, the steps forward and back. Healing went in various directions for me. It was not a straight or continuous path. I will also share the resources and what I learned from the various directions God took me. The abuse I experienced resulted in guilt, shame, unforgiveness, and a lack of trust. What is unique about the story is not what happened—unfortunately many have had this kind of experience as part of their story—what is unique is the path God took me on to heal, restoring me by replacing darkness in my heart with His love. I will share the experience when God closed the doors on all the residual feelings, doubts, hurts, and how for the first time in my life I can say, "I am free."

In many ways this is a story no one wants to read or hear. You see, I will share the deepest, darkest, and most painful experiences on my journey to healing. However, this book is not about shock and awe. It is about being real and being honest in the hopes that someone, somewhere, will connect with the words and then connect with God for a good housecleaning.

None of this story is prescriptive. It is not a formula for others to follow. It is simply my experience and my new understanding of life with God. I don't believe there is a right way to go through healing from this or any other kind of suffering. However, there has been one constant. My Father, Jesus Christ, and the Holy Spirit are with me every step of the way. I am never alone, just like He promises. "Be strong and courageous. Do not be afraid or terrified because of them, for the LORD your God goes with you; he will never leave you nor forsake you" (Deuteronomy 31:6). I may not have always felt His closeness or heard all the whisperings, but I clung to Him for dear life. And in the end, it was He who washed me clean.

Why should all of us clean house? The obvious reason is that God wants our entire heart and not just part of it. He wants to cleanse us of all that has cluttered our life and hindered our relationship with Him. He wants to free our soul (mind, will, and emotions) from the burdens we have been carrying, making room for Him to move from our head to our heart. He offers a new sense of wholeness and being loved that only comes from an open heart. I must admit I spent many years, even decades, with God in my head. I had faith, but it was logical in my head and not my heart. He wants our hearts.

It is my prayer that as you read this book you see God and not pain and struggle. I also pray that you see light and hope from a God who loves you very much, and that you see God's consistent, unending, unconditional love, along with His support and presence. I don't doubt that it is His desire to bring healing and wholeness to everyone who calls on His name.

At the end of the tour, I have chocolate chip cookies to share. Then maybe we can chat. I would love to hear your story too. I learn so much from others. But most of all, when you are done, I hope you are encouraged to clean your house. Shall we begin?

Chapter 1

Cleaning House:
Don't turn a deaf ear

When we clean house, we occasionally have to really get down into the nooks and crannies to do some deep cleaning. This is not everyday cleaning, just light mopping and vacuuming. No, once in a while, we need to get below the surface, although surface cleaning is my favorite way to go.

You might ask yourself, "Why would anyone want to put themselves through that?" I have to admit, I didn't know what I was in for. God, in His wisdom, knew I couldn't handle the big picture of everything He'd planned for me. All I knew was that I didn't like how I felt inside, and I wanted that to change. There seemed to be a dark shadow looming over my life constantly, and I was beginning to think happiness was something I'd never really experience for myself—that it was reserved for others. My prayers became desperate: "I don't know how to do this, Lord. Please help me." Thank God that He took those prayers seriously and began cleaning my house!

John 15:1-4 says:

I am the true vine, and my Father is the gardener. He cuts off every branch in me that bears no fruit, while every branch that does bear fruit He prunes, so that it will be even more fruitful. You are already clean because of the word I have spoken to you. Remain in me, as I also remain in you. No branch can bear fruit by itself; it must remain in the vine. Neither can you bear fruit unless you remain in me.

He began cutting away what was dead within me, everything from bitterness to anger. Once the dead, rotten, dried-out, strangling debris was gone, He moved to pruning so I could bear fruit; and He's still pruning away today.

When we choose God, we invite Him to be our gardener, our housecleaner. We do not have to experience abuse to need pruning. If we're being honest with ourselves, we'll see that all of us have portions of our heart that aren't brimming with love for others. These ugly, dead things usually spew out of us at the most uncontrollable moments; anger, hurtful sarcasm, and negativity are usually followed by regret and shame. Wouldn't it be great if we were able to control it or, better yet, not experience it at all? Let Him prune! If we let Him clean house, we will gain a heart filled with love for others, a heart overflowing in a way we have never experienced. He did it for me, and He's willing and wanting to do it for you. I'm sharing my story with you here, so that you can see where it all started.

The Story

The story really began a few months before I had any indication that I had something to remember. Curt and I had chosen to move in together. It was a difficult decision for me, one I never thought I'd make. In fact, the first time he asked me about it, I said, "No, simply not an option." I'd been living with my parents, and my asthma was getting worse, due to the mold in their basement. I'd weighed all of my options, though, and there weren't very many for me as a full-time graduate student. So, when Curt made the suggestion, I was extremely conflicted, torn between doing the right thing from a Christian perspective or doing the right thing for my health. Moving in with him before marriage was something I had vowed I'd never do, yet everything inside me was screaming that it was what I wanted to do. My underlying insecurities had me in constant fear that our relationship was going to fall apart. Marriage was the goal, but we both knew there were areas we had to work on before walking down the aisle to make such a commitment. I felt a sense of desperation, coupled with fear of letting God and my parents down by not doing what a good Christian girl should do. Ultimately, I listened to my wants and used my lungs as an excuse, and I moved in with Curt.

Shortly after I moved in with him, I jumped in the car and drove to Nashville to visit friends. I really needed the time in the car to be alone with God. Somewhere in Illinois, I heard it, as clear as a bell. God said, "You are exactly where you need to be…and I didn't promise you this was going to be easy." Don't get me wrong: I am not condoning that couples should live together before marriage, and I don't think that is what God wants. However, I do believe that in my case, God did something He's very, very good at: He took the situation I'd created, the choice I'd made, and made the most of it. He knew the decisions I was going to make, and He knew how to use even those ill-conceived decisions for His good. God knew that walking through that tumultuous time together would only strengthen our marriage that happened 18 months later. As I made that long drive, alone in my car with God, I began to really turn my ear toward Him, and only a month later, it all started.

At twenty-eight years old, I worked as the fitness director at a health club, between youth ministry positions at that time. God is so smart! He knew it would be hard, if not impossible, for me to really be proactive and effective in ministry when my own healing process was just beginning. It was nine months before I returned to ministry. I had served in youth ministry for almost ten years up to that point and had worked with several girls who'd been abused. I'd never really figured out why young, troubled girls seemed to gravitate to me, and I assumed they saw something in me that I didn't understand yet myself. That, however, was all about to change.

I was sitting in the office at the health club one day, on the phone with my homeopathist (one who practices a type of holistic medicine that focuses on healing from the inside out, emotionally and physically). She and I had been working together for several months. I served as her personal trainer, while she did what she could to help me improve my asthmatic condition. While my lungs were growing stronger, it was also time for me to heal emotionally, and I was checking in with her to see if we should change my remedy, the tonic or tablet I could take to move me toward better health. She asked me a question she'd asked many times before, to the point of making me angry: "Do you have any negative thoughts regarding your childhood?" My answer was always the same, a resounding, "No!" As far as I knew, all my childhood memories were positive ones.

I could remember back to the age of two. It had just finished raining on a hot summer day. I clearly remember going into the bedroom to put on my favorite bathing suit, a little pink velvet one. I then ran outside and asked Dad if I could play in the puddle at the bottom of the driveway. I had a lot of memories like this, all positive. Looking back now, I can say it is truly amazing that God has equipped us with brains that are so dead set on protecting us.

This time when she asked, though, it was different. The all-too-familiar question spawned a rush of darkness. It washed over me, starting at my head and flowing all the way down to my feet; I literally felt it move down my body. My heart knew immediately how to answer her: "I don't want to go to sleep tonight." When she asked me why, I said, "I'm afraid I'm going to remember something I don't want to remember." I was filled with panic and began to cry, and she instructed me to come by her house and pick up something to ease my anxiety. I left work right away and headed straight to her house for the homeopathic remedy.

It was strange, almost surreal. I didn't have any solid memories yet, but my heart knew I'd been sexually scarred, and I also knew, deep down, who the culprit was. I already knew the "icky neighbor" had done awful things to his daughters. I'd always felt uncomfortable around him, and I never liked being at their house when he was home. I had never mentioned to my parents that he walked around his house naked when I was there or that he let his "friend," as he called that part of his body, hang out of his shorts when he was working in his yard. His wife provided daycare for me when I was two and three years old. I was keenly aware that he'd hurt his daughters, and I always wondered why he hadn't hurt me, when he had ample opportunity. On this day, I instantly realized—as if I'd known all along—that he had done just that.

After I picked up the remedy, I ran home to Mom. In hysterics, I told her what I knew. She didn't know what to do. I know she didn't want to believe it, and since I didn't have any actual memories to go on, she could only hope it was something my imagination had drummed up, that it wasn't the least bit true. I told her immediately that I didn't blame her or Dad, because I really didn't. They would never have left me in the neighbor's care if they'd had the slightest suspicion that I wasn't safe. Because I never had spoken up, they really had no way of knowing what was going on next door. Mom asked me not to tell Dad because she worried what such grim news might do to him, and I agreed, at least for the time being.

The remedy for anxiety worked quickly, and as I calmed down, I determined that I truly wanted to be in control of the memories that were hazily coming back to me. I didn't want to endure nightmares and flashbacks like so many of the girls I'd counseled. I contacted a pastor, friend, and mentor of mine who'd been trained in the use of meditation, and I asked her to help me remember in an environment where I could feel safe. She agreed, and we set up a time to meet within the next couple of days.

That night, I told Curt. We'd been dating for about a year and a half, and we knew marriage was in our future. He was as shocked as my mother, but he made it clear that he'd support me in whatever I needed to do to get past it. The poor guy had no idea what he was in for!

Thanks to the new remedy, I was able to sleep that night

without fear or nightmares, but daylight brought a bout of depression that quickly set in. I was just numb inside, unable to feel anything. It was as if my entire world had been turned upside down in a flash.

When the time of my first meditation session finally came, I was anxious and just wanted to get it over with, to discover what had really happened to me. By focusing on the pastor's words as she invited me to imagine a safe place, I was put in a relaxed state. She didn't guide my thoughts or coach me in any way; she simply asked what I was seeing.

I told her I was about three years old, in my backyard, hiding behind the maple tree. I could see the apple tree my dad and I had planted, as well as the neighbor's house. It was warm, and the sun was shining. He was a shadow at first, but then I could see his face. He told me he did it out of love. Ick! *How can it be love?* I wondered, and that was all I remembered in that first session.

Over the next couple of sessions, the memories became clearer. He came into the room were I was napping on the bottom bunk, and I suddenly recalled why I always begged to sleep on the top bunk; I thought it would be safer up there, where he couldn't get to me as easily. He had just come home from work. I was wearing a jumper his wife had made for me, and it had snaps between the legs for easier potty breaks. He unsnapped the jumper, lifted it up, and began touching me all over. He took my panties off and—well, you get the idea.

At two and a half, my innocence was lost, my ability to trust forever tainted. After that, I'd make choices in my life without memories to rely on, without really understanding why. I would spend the next twenty-six years of life feeling I had to do everything right to make up for being like the bad little girl. Not one area of my life went unaffected by what he did that afternoon, even though it had taken me all those years to remember the root of my problems.

Memories

I must make a disclaimer regarding false memories, as a lot of controversy exists in the field of psychology regarding them. There is no question that false memories can be suggested by others or created in one's mind. However, forgetting a traumatic event is a common way to deal with shame and guilt.

Dr. Dan Allender does a good job of unpacking this in his book, *The Wounded Heart*. He refers to it as "suppression" rather than "repression" and says, "I believe the process of 'blocking memories' at any age arises out of confusion, horror, shame, and/or sorrow." According to Dr. Allender, suppression is when one actively holds something back, and this has consequences. One is the hardening of the heart, and another is moral blindness. He encourages us to face areas in which we've put our trust in something or someone other than God. This is what is primary, not the memory recovery itself. He also states that memories help us see when we've fled from God and tried to live without God. They help us understand why we don't trust God.

This has been true for me. When those memories resurfaced, they helped me understand many decisions I made and emphasized how I closed my heart to God by not trusting Him or feeling worthy of His love. The logical response of a young child when an adult violates his or her trust is simply not to trust anyone. At that age, I didn't understand long-term effects.

Once I understood why I'd felt so broken, it was finally time to put the pieces back together, and I wanted to feel whole again—to feel happy and laugh. I didn't know what was ahead of me, but I knew God would get me through. My prayers turned into my begging God to get me through it quickly, and I knew He would. Honestly, though, I did not have a sense of peace that surpassed all understanding or a supernatural strength to carry on. I felt as if I were in the bottom of some dark and horrible pit, and I wanted out. I still remembered what life was like out of the pit, but as much as I wanted out, I didn't know if I had the strength to climb out. It took all the strength I had to just ask God for help. I didn't hear any guidance or reassurance because I hadn't yet postured myself to listen; depression will do that to a person. In fact, I thought all my education and training would enable me to heal myself, and that was the epitome of foolishness.

It didn't take long for my homeopathist to suggest that I see a psychologist. I didn't want to go and didn't think I needed to, but when I resisted, she exercised a bit of tough love and said she'd withhold my next remedy until I made an appointment. Really having no other choice, I called the next day to set up the appointment. My wise homeopathist also suggested that I tell the intake person why I was in need of an appointment. I was a graduate student at the time, so my healthcare was covered by the university system, and she advised me that telling them my reason for going there would ensure that the counseling center would connect me with the right therapist for my specific problem. In the end, she was right. It was time to start healing, time to face what God was showing me, and I could no longer turn a deaf ear.

That was just the beginning of my journey to clean out all

the dark places and illuminate them with the light of God's love. There has been some serious deep cleaning, as well as some light touchups along the way. When we are deep cleaning, we have to know everything that needs to be done so we know where to start. Creating a to-do list is a good first step. The list might be long and feel overwhelming, but don't worry! "All things are possible" through God. He can handle it, and so can we.

Getting started can be the one of the most difficult parts of cleaning house. Like any other daunting task, it's best to take it in bite-sized chunks. It can't be done in one day, so we must start with what we can manage today and continue moving forward, one step at a time. Once we are moving, it is easier to keep going. So, my friend, grab your cleaning supplies, and let's get started!

As we work through this together, remember that my advice here is based on how God took me through the process of cleaning my house; your approach maybe a little different than mine. To put it in housecleaning terms, I might prefer Pine-Sol to your Mr. Clean! The goal, however, is the same: We cannot turn a deaf ear to what God is showing us. We all want our house to be sparkling clean and organized, with everything in its place, so the essentials are clear and uncluttered. Deep cleaning is hard work that requires lots of time and energy and even occasional breaks. Cleaning house is a lifelong process, and we won't be entirely finished until we are done in this life; however, once the tough stuff is done, maintenance is much easier.

James 1:2-5 tells us,

Consider it pure joy, my brothers, whenever you face trials of many kinds, because you know that the testing of your faith develops perseverance. Perseverance must finish its work so that you may be mature and complete, not lacking anything. If any of you lacks wisdom, he should ask God, who gives generously to all without finding fault, and it will be given to him."

I encourage you to ask God to guide you and reveal where He wants you to start cleaning. I also encourage you to posture yourself so that you may clearly hear what God wants to reveal. Not all of us are ready to take what God has for us and make the changes necessary for the seeds He is planting so that we may grow and prosper. As the parable of the sower tells us in Matthew 13, sometimes the seeds fall on the soil, but without proper nourishment, those seeds won't grow. We may hear what we need to do and understand it without being ready to move forward. Sometimes the seeds fall on rocks, like deaf ears. We cannot hear what God is trying to tell us at all. And sometimes the seeds land in the thorns. We aren't able to hear clearly what God is saying because thorns are in the way and prevent us from hearing the full message.

When we feel stuck, it helps to ask God to show us where the block is. Often, when we ask, we'll suddenly have a sense of knowing about the issue, and I trust that knowing comes from God. God's timing and ours need to be one and the same, so the seeds will prosper. I spent years turning a deaf ear toward God, but when I finally began to listen, my life began to change in remarkable ways. He has more to show me, but it all started with cleaning the closets.

Chapter 2

Cleaning Closets:
Get rid of historical junk

When we clean house, there are areas we tend to ignore because they are too much work. When God cleans house, He gets behind those closed doors. When I know people are coming over, I shove junk into drawers and closets, close them tight, and hope no one opens them. Out of sight, out of mind, right? As a result, I have years, even decades of junk in my closets, and it's exactly that historical junk that God wants to dig out of our lives.

We know that cleaning closets is hard work that we dread. We might have to set aside a full day or two to get the job done. It takes a long time, and we have to make a big mess to get to the end result. To further prepare for what we might find, we bring in garbage bags and containers to sort all the stuff. Then we take a deep breath and dive into what seems like never-ending piles of junk and stuff and debris.

I start by pulling everything out. When I do, I find things I haven't seen in years. I lay it all out on the floor and the bed. Some things are junk that I don't want or need in my life anymore. Those things go straight into the garbage bag. Some things make me pause and reflect about certain memories. Some of those memories are sad and make me cry, while others bring laughter. Things look differently to me now than when I first stuffed those things in the closet. When I come across wrinkled or yellowed things, I flatten them out and ponder if they should stay or go into the garbage. God gives me new insights about the historical junk that allows me to let it go.

Finally, when everything is out of the closet, I look at the mountain of stuff I had crammed into such a small space. What a mess! I'm often amazed how much I manage to collect and tuck away, and much of it was forgotten about. I have to ask myself, *Who was I saving it for or hiding it from?*

Once the closet is clear, it's time to reorganize. I begin putting the stuff back, making sure there's a place for everything worth keeping. Some things need to be hung up, so I can grab them at a moment's notice. Some things go in new containers, labeled with new meaning, and are tucked way in the back of the closet. I need to hang on to them but they don't need to be in the forefront anymore. As I reminisce longer, God shows me a few more things I can let go of and put in the trash. Everything I need to keep goes back in, organized and neat, and the garbage is disposed of. It feels good, almost therapeutic. I feel lighter when I get rid of so much historical junk, and there's even some empty space left in the closet that can be filled up with new and better things such as joy and love.

Healing Begins

The first time I heard the lyrics from Michael W. Smith's "Healing Rain," I sobbed. I still can't listen to that song without tearing up. Why? Because there's something scary about accepting the healing that is poured out by the Holy Spirit. It's difficult to give up what I know and accept that life can be different—or at least that's been true for me. That kind of "healing rain" can come in different forms, and it can take a long time to completely transform one's heart from brokenness to wholeness. For me, it happened in pieces and stages, so I'm a bit envious of those who receive instant healing from God. That would have been much easier, but it was not His plan for me.

Emotional and spiritual healing is a scary concept to many, and it most definitely was for me. The unknown, un-certainty of what would lie ahead, caused anxiety within me. While I thought therapy must be a great option for other people, I was under the impression that I should have been able to heal myself. I'd certainly had enough education and training. My parents taught me to be independent and take care of myself, and I assumed I should be able to get off the couch and change the way I felt. The thing is, clinical depres-sion doesn't work that way. It took every ounce of strength I had to get up and do a load of laundry. Curt was beginning to wonder if he would ever see me smile again. I dedicated the little positive emotion I could muster to my clients at the gym, which meant there was nothing left for Curt or anyone else by the end of the day.

Depression can become comfortable, like getting used to the pile of junk in the corner of the room. I knew it needed to be dealt with, but I didn't want to take the time to do it. I was getting used to how I felt. *Could this become my new normal? Could this be what life will be like from now on?* I wondered. Ignoring it or pretending it hadn't happened at all both seemed like good options to me. Living with depression seemed easier than dealing with the pains of my past. But a small voice inside kept telling me I didn't want to feel like that anymore. It was faint but I clung to it anyway, and I was still certain I could deal with it on my own. But who was I kidding? Only myself!

I knew that healing would mean facing the abuse head on. I would have to look it right in the eye, and I wasn't ready to do that. To get started, I began working through a book, *The Sexual Healing Journey*, by Wendy Maltz, which was recommended by a friend. It became a great resource for me primarily because it allowed me to feel normal in what I was experiencing. It was also a great tool to help me sort and organize all the stuff that continued to run through my head. I was able to pull out the emotions and reactions related to abuse and put them in a separate box, while placing relationship stuff in another. One chapter of that book is dedicated to handling things with significant others. When I couldn't find the words or strength to say what was on my heart, I asked Curt to read from that section of the book. I was hoping that wonderful book would be enough to let me heal myself, but that wasn't the case. I was making progress, but I needed guidance from a professional. As my homeopathist had said, I needed therapy.

Once I accepted that, off I went to my first therapy appointment, though I had a chip on my shoulder and told the therapist, flat out, that I had no desire to be there. Her reaction was to tell me I might not be ready to start therapy yet. That made me angry; I told her it wasn't an option because as much as I didn't want to be there, I knew it was the only way I could stop feeling what I was feeling. I'd started to see therapy as a way out of the depression, an exit from the blah, icky feeling that was eating me up inside. I would force myself to follow through with it for that reason.

The therapist made her official diagnosis: post-traumatic stress disorder (PTSD) and depression, and she suggested we meet every two weeks for the foreseeable future. She also said I qualified for antidepressants. I didn't want to use medication, as long as my PTSD and depression wasn't so bad that I couldn't go to work and accomplish basic tasks. Frankly, I was afraid that if I started to feel better with medication, I'd become dependent on it and would just stay on it and give up working on getting to the root of the problem. Medicine is a great option for many people, sometimes the only option, but I wanted to try to conquer my depression without it. So, as it turned out, that first appointment was rather unsatisfying.

Initially I dreaded going to therapy. I wasn't seeing any progress, so it seemed pointless. However, as I began to share more and more about the memories and what I was experiencing day to day, I began to feel comfortable with the process. I began to actually build a trusting relationship with my therapist. After several sessions, I actually started looking forward to my discussions with her. It became a safe place to let my emotions out. Being able to sort my emotions out in therapy meant they weren't bogging me down as much day to day. I began to smile more and found some peace. I guess you could say therapy became my garbage dump and recycling center. My therapist helped me see what needed to go into the trash and what just needed to be reorganized and put back in a different place, maybe with a different label on it.

I was also finding that I had more energy for work and Curt. I finally began to see a light at the end of that very long tunnel. On the flipside, I knew I could get comfortable there, that therapy could go on forever without making any real progress. Chatting and even venting to my therapist was fine, but I had to ask, "Am I really getting anywhere?" It was like shuffling piles around on the bed without putting anything back. It was time for me to get to work on putting things in the closet. I was finally ready to close the door on that closet, and I didn't want to look back in there for a very long time.

At my next appointment, I shared my concerns and mentioned that I needed to see progress. I needed to do more than just dump my emotions twice a month. I needed to set goals so I could see when I was moving forward. I needed to see that therapy was going to end someday. Something internal was pushing me forward. My therapist listened to me, as usual, and rose to the task by giving me homework assignments. On a side note, many therapists are trained to let the patient guide the sessions. We need to feel empowered to ask for what we need. Therapists are not mind-readers, though it might feel that way at times. We need to listen to that still, small voice of the Holy Spirit within us that's moving us forward. It is so easy to ignore our guide. What I didn't see at the time was that God was burning the junk through the entire process.

One thing my therapist asked was if Curt would be willing to come in for a session or two, if needed; and he was willing, even though she never actually invited him to come in. She also recommended that I begin a journal. I hated writing and still do. Truth be told, there are only about ten entries in that journal. As few as there are, however, when I reread them, I saw that they were quite significant. In the end, the journal was a useful tool for it helped me externalize all I was carrying around. At one point, I struggled with a lot of anger raging inside. At times, I felt completely out of control. I wrote about one of these experiences in my journal:

> Today I got extremely angry at this girl at work for no reason. I raged on the inside. I'm sure my face let on. I really had a hard time containing it. I am afraid I'm about to lose it. I don't care if I get angry at the icky neighbor, but I don't want to get angry at somebody for nothing. Curt said I could take it out on him. What a guy!

I told Curt he could read my journal anytime or ask me anything about what happened or what I was going through. At one point, I used the journal to tell him some things I was having trouble saying out loud. There were things in the relationship box that needed to be dealt with. I didn't want to hurt him, but there were issues I was having with our relationship that he needed to know about. I knew that if our relationship was going to survive, I couldn't shut him out of what I was experiencing. The journal was a safe way for me to share my heart. In it I wrote what I wanted to say and then asked him to read it. When he did, he began to have a better understanding of what I was experiencing.

Truthfully, I was terrified he'd break up with me. My emotions were on a rollercoaster. I wasn't nice to him; I felt like damaged goods. I thought for sure he'd eventually tire of dealing with me and my junk and want out. I'm sure he wanted my junk back in the closet too. It's one thing to deal with your own mess, but it's another when it is someone else's mess. But grace entered the picture through Curt. He assured me he wouldn't go anywhere as long as I was working on healing. What a gift! I really needed to hear that, and it powered me on toward healing. Over the years, his love and support has taught me a lot about grace.

Next, it was time to write a letter to the icky neighbor; my therapist told me it would help me get the abuse box put back on the shelf in the back corner of the closet. My assignment was to put everything I had ever wanted to say to him on paper and bring the letter back with me to my next appointment. When I did, my therapist asked me to picture the icky neighbor in the chair next to me so I could read the letter to him. It was a very powerful moment, and it started me on the path to forgiveness.

I read to that vision of my abuser:

> Icky Neighbor… Somehow or another, I really believe you meant me no harm, but you violated me. You touched me sexually, and you had no right. You took away my voice and my ability to speak out when I feel threatened. Because of you, I have nightmares, crying spells, flashbacks, total sadness, and a complete void inside. You made me a confused teen, not knowing what was okay and what wasn't. You have caused me more pain than any human should have to endure. And, what really sucks is that you walk free. The only way for you to pay for pain you have caused to your family and me is for you to hurt another young child and get caught. If that's the only way, I'd rather you walk free. I know I can put the pieces of my life back together, but what about your daughters? I know I should be screaming angry at you, and sometimes I am, but mostly, my heart breaks. —*Mary*.

That was the beginning of healing for me, and only a

couple months afterwards, I told my therapist I thought I was done with therapy. She agreed, for I'd worked through everything that had presented itself. She cautioned me that something else might come to the surface, particularly when I had my own children, and that I might need to return to therapy then.

I told everyone I'd graduated from therapy, but I made sure Curt knew he had the right to tell me if he felt I needed to go back. I figured he would recognize it before I would, or at least he'd acknowledge it first. I hopefully thought that would be the end of dealing with the abuse, but it was really only the beginning. I'd been wounded, and there were many more layers to peel off to bring me into the fullness of God's purpose and plan for me. There was more closet-cleaning in my future. I eventually learned that closet-cleaning is easier when we understand what a wound really is and how it continues to affect our lives.

Conclusion

Much of my closet-cleaning took place in traditional talk therapy, a great way to sort out and organize my thoughts and emotions. But as we learned in Hebrews 12:25-29, ultimate cleansing requires God's revelation in our heart. Only God can remove the historical junk and replace it with His love.

Chapter 3

Cleaning Closets: With God

My early closet-cleaning really consisted of me doing what I thought I was supposed to be doing, with God's help. When I finally wised up and let God lead the cleaning—wow! All I can say is that He really knows what He's doing. I began to experience a freedom and wholeness I didn't even know was possible. My ability to love God, self, and others increased dramatically. My self-confidence was also boosted, and the list of other benefits could go on. I felt myself becoming the person I'd always thought I was supposed to be; before, I just didn't know how to get there. I have to warn you that some of the cleaning might be a little abrasive; in my case, it stung, but it was well worth it.

Wounding

All of us have buried wounds in our closets. As we unpack and reorganize, God may begin to reveal to us areas where a wound changed our thinking about ourselves and others, Himself included. As He shows us these things, we can put them in the garbage and get them out of our closet for good.

I had been wounded and had been cast into a cycle of private pain and wounding others. I had built walls around myself for protection from further hurt, but there was a longing and emptiness inside. I expected others to fill the hole, but only God can fill such a void. I was given a new understanding of wounding, which helped me allow God to fill the emptiness that had begun to feel normal. Since I'd graduated from therapy, I thought I was finally feeling normal; I was so used to it that I wasn't even aware of all the holes in my heart. I harbored this sense that I was dirty, and I assumed that everyone felt that way. God began to show me the sense of wholeness that I could have through Him. Before that, I didn't know it was even possible.

A physical wound is usually easy to identify and treat medically. Emotional wounds, however, are trickier. It is not always obvious that the source of our negative emotions is a past wound. These wounds can leave a person feeling defiled, tormented, and grieved. Lesser wounds are more like an abrasion or scratch; they hurt but don't linger. Some wounds trigger older, deeper wounds; these are noticeable when someone frets or feels like something is festering. Sometimes wounds act like lesions that keep breaking open and won't heal. It is natural to want to hide or bury wounds. The problem is they are buried alive and continue to thrive under the surface, bringing harm, both emotionally and physically.

We have all been wounded, as hurts are a part of life. What we do with those wounds and how we react to them can either move us further into darkness or toward the light of God's love. The problem is that many of us react to life out of our woundedness without any thought as to why we behave the way we do. How often do we make decisions out of fear or shame? According to Dr. Colbert, if we dwell on old hurts and wounds over time, we end up building a mental habit. In other words, a stress response will occur more quickly each time we allow the old emotions to resurface. Not only does one suffer emotionally, but the increase of stress hormones also does physical damage.

Childhood sexual abuse isn't the only wound I have experienced, but it was the beginning of a cycle of pain I was living in, without even being aware of it. It changed the way I internalized my experiences and limited my ability to receive love from family and God, due to the lack of trust it caused. I always thought, *This is just who I am.* I learned at a very young age not to trust, and I decided that if I couldn't trust adults, I certainly couldn't trust God. This wounding also began a cycle of pain, and I kept telling myself in subtle ways that I was unworthy of love, respect, or financial gain.

Shiloh Place Ministries helped me unpack this during a prayer ministry training event. A wound, or "love deficit," as they call it, leads to negative thinking. This, in turn, leads to sin (unforgiveness, judging), which then leads to darkness (strongholds, isolation, and independence), which leads to oppression, and ultimately goes back to wounding.

Here is an example: When I was a child, I carried a little extra weight, while all of my friends were stick thin. Because other children often remarked about my weight, I felt like I was fifty pounds heavier than everyone else, even though I was only about ten pounds heavier than my best friend at the time. Their comments hurt, but I was able to blow them off at first. Then those wounds led to negative thoughts about being unlovable and unwanted. From there, when I began to believe the awful things they said, I turned to food for comfort; as a child, it never occurred to me to turn to God for comfort. This brought darkness into my heart and left an open door for the enemy. As the cycle continued, the seed of unworthiness began to grow, a seed I believe was planted during the abuse. Turning to food for comfort became a habit, one that has been very hard to break.

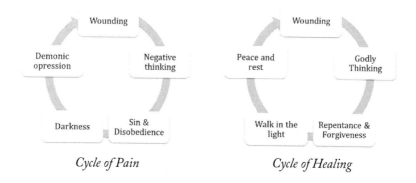

Cycle of Pain   Cycle of Healing

We can slowly change our thinking patterns and replace the cycle of pain with a cycle of healing. (Diagrams are from the curriculum *The Turning* by Agape Christian Family Church.) Instead of allowing pain, we must catch the negative or ungodly thought, which can be the most difficult part. Once we catch those thoughts, we can change them into God's truth. We can repent for the ungodly belief and shine God's light into that area and, in exchange for all that negativity, receive God's peace.

Are there areas in which you know you're operating out of a cycle of pain? Do you have an abnormal response to common situations? Sometimes these are referred to as "buttons." Ask your spouse or kids, as I'm sure they are keenly aware of your buttons, which often sprout up from wounds that are unhealed. As you clean your closets and sort through those wounds you have buried deep down inside, ask God to show you where He wants to begin in bringing you healing. God often reminds me that there are layers to healing. Sometimes, just when I think an issue has been dealt with, it suddenly comes back. This is usually because there is another level of healing God wants to bring to me. Unworthiness is one area that is being peeled like an onion for me. As we continue our housecleaning, we will further unpack this cycle and examine it more closely.

Forgiveness

To truly get rid of historical junk, forgiveness is often necessary. As I cleaned out my closet, certain memories brought out rage, pain, and floods of tears. God showed me it was time to forgive the icky neighbor. As I worked through this, my forgiveness of him only took place in my heart. I haven't seen or had contact with him since the memories returned, and he had moved out of my parents' neighborhood years before that.

Sometimes putting things in the forgiveness box can be the hardest part of closet-cleaning, but this is important clutter to put away. It can be very heavy and cumbersome, which means it interferes in many parts of our lives.

Let me begin by saying what forgiveness is not. Forgiveness is not letting the person off the hook, and it is not about finding some redeeming quality in them. It does not eliminate the need for consequences, nor does it suggest that what the person did was okay. The person who wounded me doesn't have to ask me for forgiveness. In fact, this is not about the person who wounded me. Rather, it is a position of my heart. Forgiveness is also not a cleansing or minimalization, in any way, of the shame and pain caused by the wound, but we will deal with that later.

Forgiveness is deciding to let go of resentment, bitterness, or anger as a result of a perceived offense. It is definitely easier to hold on to it than it is to let go. But why should we forgive those who've wounded us? We forgive for our sake not theirs. Dr. Colbert, in *Deadly Emotions*, writes, "Forgiveness releases layers of hurt and heals the raw edges of emotional pain" (p. 163). He also cites a study from the University of Wisconsin, "The Forgiveness Study," which found that learning to forgive can actually prevent heart disease (p.169). Unforgiveness has been linked to autoimmune diseases, arthritis, MS, thyroid disease, lupus, ulcerative colitis, and more—all on top of the deep emotional pain of grudges that we cannot seem to let go of.

We mustn't forget the most important reason to forgive, and Colossians 3:13 reminds us, "Bearing with one another and forgiving each other, if anyone has a complaint against any, even as Christ forgave you, so you do also."

And just how many times should we forgive someone? Jesus tells us in Matthew 18 to forgive seventy times seven. That's a tall order! Luke 6:13 says, "Do not judge, and you will not be judged. Do not condemn, and you will not be condemned. Forgive, and you will be forgiven." Jesus says it over and over: We need to forgive others to receive forgiveness. In Matthew 6:14-15, *The Amplified Bible*, which takes the Greek and expands upon it, says, "For if you forgive people their trespasses [their reckless and willful sins, leaving them, letting them go, and giving up resentment], your Heavenly Father will also forgive you. But if you do not forgive others their trespasses [their reckless and willful sins, leaving them, letting them go, and giving up resentment], neither will your Father forgive you your trespasses."

We can take from this that we are to forgive both reckless (accidental) and willful trespasses (those done on purpose). This goes even further, defining forgiveness as leaving, letting go, and giving up resentment. Yes, you are reading it correctly. If we don't forgive others, our Father will not forgive us. Ouch! This is part of scripture that far too often overlooked because it is difficult to believe that a loving Father would refuse to forgive us, but to reiterate this point, we can turn to Mark 11:24-26:

> *Therefore I tell you, whatever you ask for in prayer, believe that you have received it, and it will be yours. And when you stand praying, if you hold anything against anyone, forgive him, so that your Father in Heaven may forgive you your sins. But if you do not forgive, neither will your Father who is in Heaven forgive your sins.*

God knows that if we hold unforgiveness in our heart, we have put up a wall between Him and us. Psychologists refer to this as a "defense mechanism," an unconscious reaction to something or someone we perceive as a threat. When we have been wounded, we begin to build a wall of self-defense around ourselves. We stop letting people know our deepest thoughts and feelings, for fear of rejection. When we stop letting others in, we stop letting God in; and darkness, anger, bitterness, and resentment all get in the way of us accepting His love. When I realized that I'd closed my heart to God, thinking I was merely protecting myself, I was stunned. I had unknowingly pushed God away! I had to let it go to let God into my heart, and that started with forgiveness. There is freedom in forgiveness.

This was a hot topic in a Bible study I led a few years ago. One woman described a family rift that had gone on for years. She had kept all the letters she'd received, as well as copies of the ones she sent. She used those as weapons, her evidence of how right she was when everyone else was so wrong. In doing so, she drummed up all that anger and resentment again and gave it new life. Every time she revisited the letters, her negative emotions flooded back to the surface. Every so often, the scab would get picked, and the wound would be reopened. One day, though, God—in His infinite wisdom—opened her eyes to forgiveness. As an act of letting go, she tore up every one of the letters. Years of letters were in shreds on the floor around her, and a huge weight had been lifted off her. Her heart was forever changed, and her capacity for love increased. Why? Because she finally cleaned out a closet!

Like her, I was finally able to forgive the icky neighbor, and that was a huge step forward in my healing. When all that anger and bitterness was released, it allowed more room for God in my heart. Most of us won't hear our perpetrators ask for forgiveness. Remember, the forgiveness I'm speaking of here is about releasing the anger and resentment from our hearts; in no way does forgiveness release the person from responsibility or consequences. It does not mean you wish to share a relationship with that person who has wronged you. It does not make the offense okay. I finally came to realize an important truth: Hurt people hurt people, and that realization gave a whole new meaning to forgiving those who know not what they do. Now I am out to stop this cycle of pain and wounding. I wanted to stop hurting myself and others, so the next step was to forgive. That allowed me to stop the ungodly lies, those thought patterns I'd bought into, and replace them with God's truth and light. That was the beginning of forgiveness for me. Since then, God has revealed other areas where I need to forgive and let go. It continues to be a painful but freeing process.

Because it's so difficult and painful, you might be asking, "How do we do it?" First, we must choose it. Remember that it is not natural, not part of our human nature. We must willfully claim it. Write in a journal: "I first ask God to forgive my unwillingness to forgive." Then tell God that you choose now to forgive and replace the pain and anger with His light and love. Ask God to help you continue letting go. When I find myself heading back to the anger and resentment, I remind myself, *Hey! You already let this go, remember?* Forgiveness is a choice that takes courage, and sometimes we have to choose it over and over to be able to walk in the freedom of it. Remember these words from the Apostle Paul in Ephesians 4:31-32:

> *Get rid of all bitterness, rage, and anger, brawling and slander, along with every form of malice. 32Be kind and compassionate to one another, forgiving each other, just as, in Christ, God forgave you.*

Some people think forgiveness is the end of the healing, but that hasn't been my experience. Forgiveness is a good way to attack the root of the problem; however, it does not get rid of the underlying pain. It didn't cleanse me of shame. Even after I was able to forgive, a residue of shame, unworthiness, and defilement still lingered in my heart. These are deeper areas of grime. In fact, I thought some of those things would be stuck in my heart forever. I needed to deal with old garbage that was lurking about in the corners of my mind if I was going to change the cycle of pain into one of healing.

One important tool I was taught was visualization, a tool that can be used in all areas of prayer. Visualization while praying is as simple as closing our eyes and creating a picture. For some, this can initially be quite difficult; but the more we work at it, the easier it gets. I started by picturing a familiar picture of Jesus. Now I picture beams of God's white light surrounding me, pouring into my heart. For me, this is a way of internalizing God's love, of moving it out of my head and into my heart. His love becomes something I can feel, not just know.

As I prayed through my unforgiveness, I visualized God's love pouring into my heart as beams of white light. I saw bits of darkness being burned away by His love, and this helped move His love into my heart. We must remember that light is always capable of displacing darkness. We can choose to hide the pain inside us, but that will limit how much of God's love can come in, and we will remain as we are. Darkness is the absence of light, but once we let that light in, we can let the pain out. To do that, we have to feel it. For some of us, a good cry is the perfect way to release pain, while others must go through a full grieving process that can take weeks. There is an entire spectrum that God can take us through. I hold on tight to the fact that He knows what I need. In the end, I always have a deeper relationship with my Father.

We have to be ready to let go of the area we're inviting God to clean out. Thankfully He knows where we are and will clean the layers as we are ready. He won't impose His love on us; we have to be ready to accept it.

The following is my prayer about forgiveness. We can

make up our own prayer for any area we need God's love to pour into. It is as simple as visualizing, repenting, asking God to take it, and inviting His love in to replace it. I prayed:

> God, I know I have had a heart of unforgiveness toward _____. Please forgive my unforgiveness. I want to be set free of it. I only want Your joy and love in my heart. I claim Your love over all areas of my life, especially the painful and difficult areas I keep beating myself up over. Your love is greater than my unforgiveness. Break my heart open, Holy Spirit! Pour Your love in and release all the darkness I've been holding on to. I know I'm feeling this pain because I have to release it to make room for Your love in my heart. Fill me, Holy Spirit. Break the unforgiveness in my heart and replace it with your amazing love. All I want is You in my heart. Praises to you, God.

Conclusion

Letting God be in control, exposing our wounds, and working on forgiveness allows us to get rid of historical junk permanently. Once that sting is gone, it's gone for good; but only if we fix our eyes and heart on Him. When I'm hurt or angry, it's difficult for me to let Him show me His way. That's when I remember Philippians 4:12b-13:

> *I have learned the secret of being content in any and every situation, whether well fed or hungry, whether living in plenty or want. I can do all this through Him who gives me strength* (TNIV).

Then I try communicating with God through my heart and not my head. Any Psalm or scripture that speaks to one's heart is a good place to start. Psalm 42 is one great example:

> *My soul thirsts for God, for the living God. When can I go and meet with God? My tears have been my food day and night, while men say to me all day long, "Where is your God?" These things I remember as I pour out my soul: how I used to go with the multitude, leading the procession to the house of God, with shouts of joy and thanksgiving among the festive throng Why are you downcast, O my soul? Why so disturbed within me? Put your hope in God, for I will yet praise Him, my Savior and my God.*

I try to be myself with God, speaking from my heart. I don't guard my sense of humor or my sarcasm. *The Shack*, by William Paul Young is a fiction work, but the book is a beautiful example of how raw honesty with God builds intimacy:

> Silence followed as Mack wrestled with what Jesus had said. He gave up after only a minute or two and decided to ask the riskier question. "You said I don't really know you. It would be a lot easier if we could always talk like this."
>
> "Admittedly, Mack this is special. You were really stuck and we wanted to help you crawl out of your pain. But don't just think that just because I'm not visible, our relationship has to be less real. It will be different, but perhaps even more real." (p. 112)

In this part of the story, Mack is just learning how to be honest with Jesus, how to ask the tough questions. As the story continues, he begins to know a God who will go to great lengths to have a relationship with him, a God who wants to be real in his life. I have learned to tell God everything that is on my heart, including why I feel the way I feel and what my heart needs. I give thanks for everything in my life, even the difficulties. I also continue to write out my thoughts in my prayer journal. I do all of this in an effort to prevent a buildup of new historical junk, and it all helps get my emotions out of my heart to make room for God to express Himself to me.

Most of us have more than one closet. Don't be surprised if somewhere down the line, you discover a new closet to clean or find one that needs reorganizing. God has a way of revealing new areas of healing to us as we draw closer to Him. I believe we are all involved in a lifelong process of cleaning, whether we realize it or not. As we daily choose healing over pain, just know that God will carry us through. Each and every day, I strive to live more of my life out of love than out of pain and wounding. Some days are easier than others, and I still slip and stumble. I still have areas of wounding to work on and habits to break, and I'm sure you do too—but we can't give up!

Chapter 4

Cleaning Behind the Fridge:
It must be cleaned

This is the cleaning no one wants to do. Thus, years, sometimes decades, go by between cleanings. In fact, I have to admit that I don't even move appliances out to clean behind them unless I have to for painting or repairs. Every time I do move them out, what I find is a disgusting mess lurking behind them—piles of unrecognizable yuckiness. This kind of cleaning requires those elbow-high rubber gloves, the kind that hunters use to field-dress a deer, or veterinarians use with very large animals, or the host of Dirty Jobs uses. This certainly qualifies as a dirty job that no one wants to do, and it takes a lot of courage and resolve. Still, it has to be done, so put on the rubber gloves and fetch a big bucket of hot water and your favorite disinfectant, because this is going to get ugly!

We have to delve into deep, dark, filthy crevices. With God, we are bigger and stronger than the gross pile of yuck in a dark, blackened corner. He wants us clean as John the Baptist states in Matthew 3:11-12:

I'm baptizing you here in the river, turning your old life in for a kingdom life. The real action comes next: The

*main character in this drama—I'm a mere stagehand—
will ignite the kingdom life within you, a fire within you,
the Holy Spirit within you, changing you from the inside
out. He's going to clean house, make a clean sweep of your
lives. He'll place everything true in its proper place before
God; everything false, He'll put out with the trash to be
burned* (MSG).

We may have to go for straight bleach. For the house to
be truly clean, we have to get serious. The best part is that
once we shine the light in those dark corners, the darkness
will dissipate, and what really needs to be clean will be revealed. This is hard work. It takes tremendous strength to
move a fridge, which is the first step. This will expose what
has been covered under darkness and will allow you to get a
clear picture of what you need to clean.

Just looking at the yuck behind the fridge can cause fear,
which often gets in the way of our willingness to go into
those dark corners. You might take a peek behind the fridge
and not want to go any further. There is a lot of fear to contend with, whether it be fear of what we will find or fear of
reality being worse than we can even imagine. Fear can be
crippling and prevent us from the fullness of God. He wants
us to be free and cleansed of sin. Remember that God's love
can cast out all fear (1 John 4:18). As we learn in Isaiah
41:10, we have to replace fear with love:

*So do not fear, for I am with you; do not be dismayed, for I
am your God. I will strengthen you and help you; I will
uphold you with my righteous right hand.*

Fear is not what God wants for us. Rather, He wants us

to cling to Him and allow Him to displace our fear with His love, but we'll talk more about that later. For now, pump up those muscles and let's stand strong in our faith in God while we pull out that fridge!

Deep, Dark Corners

This is the part God wants me to be completely open about, the part I really didn't want to write. But remember, He won't quit until everything is spic and span, so I wrote this in the hopes that it will help someone, maybe someone like you. God wants us to know that we are His precious children, no matter what we have gone through or what has gone through our minds. Yes, we have been wounded, but He wants to take away our pain. He wants to fill that aching, dark hole with His love. I feel as if I am just beginning to understand the depth and breadth of His love.

Only because God is holding me together and because He desperately wants you to know that you are okay could I commit any of this to paper to be read by the public. We cannot let fear win! He told me we have to know it's okay, so I have willingly shared here what was lurking behind my fridge, my own personal yuck.

Previously, I'd only shared this story with Curt. While our oldest son was an infant, I was changing his diaper when a fleeting thought ran through my head—a vision of me inappropriately touching my baby boy. I was horrified that such a thing could even waft across my mind, even for a second that I could even imagine it. *What kind of a monster am I?* I thought. Then I said, "Devil, be gone! You don't get me." It was not exactly a natural reaction for a girl raised in a church that didn't talk about the devil. I began to pray, "God, what's wrong with me? Please take this from me. Don't ever let me have a thought like that again. I could never hurt my son." I begged God over and over to wipe me clean of that vision.

If I read this about someone else, I'd immediately think she should be taken straight to jail, or at least an asylum of some sort. I'd be the first to cry out, "Put her away before she really hurts someone! Don't let my children—or any children—near her!" I must not be the only one who has had this kind of experience; however, because God was very adamant that I share this part of my healing story He said, "They need to know it's okay." The vision instantly provided me with an understanding of how easy it is for the cycle of abuse to continue. If God hadn't been in my life, I can't bear to think of where that fleeting thought might have taken me. What I didn't understand at the time was that it really was an open door for the enemy to work against me in my life.

I've never had a vision like that since. God took that from me because He never quits until all the filth is cleaned. Still, it did haunt me. The vision was a wound, and it began the cycle of pain all over again. I beat myself up about it in my head. *What would Curt think of me?* I questioned whether it would come back and couldn't seem to let it go. *Do I need to go back to therapy? Can I even admit this out loud to the therapist?* I continued to pray, though, and the Holy Spirit kept nudging me to tell Curt. I was certain he would say I needed to go back to therapy. I worried that he might never trust me again or, worse, that he'd demand a divorce.

Finally, when I couldn't take it anymore, I broke down and confessed to my husband, and his reply surprised me: "That seems normal based on what you've been through. I know you'd never hurt our son."

I sobbed. Again, amazing grace was shown through Curt. Just hearing those words provided relief to me, and that took all the power out of the image. I stopped obsessing about it immediately, and all fear and anxiety were gone.

I now understand that the darkness had to flee because I'd shined God's light on the secret I'd been keeping from Curt out of fear. Had I kept that secret, it would have created a dark place in my heart, one the enemy could build upon. That darkness would have grown and driven a wedge between my husband and I, and it would have likely damaged other relationships as well. Secrets do that—they push us further into deep, dark corners. I never would have stopped tormenting myself, and I believe the anxiety and fear very well might have increased to the point of possible physical or mental illness. The Holy Spirit prevented that from happening, not my own understanding. I thank God regularly for giving me enough strength to be obedient to the Holy Spirit's nudging. What the enemy tried to use against me actually strengthened my marriage and me.

There Is More

Apparently, it was time to clean behind the fridge again. Years had gone by, and out of nowhere, something inside me snapped. Curt and I were watching a movie that began with a scene in which a little girl was being abused, and I absolutely lost it. I began to cry and demanded that he turn the movie off. I've never been able to watch those scenes in movies anyway, but this incident was different than all the others. Before that, I could just close my eyes and ears or fast-forward through the parts that bothered me, and Curt offered to do that, but that wasn't enough. That time, I needed him to turn it off completely. Even though I didn't understand why my reaction was so extreme, I felt panicky inside. I curled up in a little ball, tried to shake it off, and went to sleep.

A week or so later, after Curt and I had been intimate, I began to sob uncontrollably. I knew something was wrong. Again, I curled up in a little ball and didn't want him to touch me. Something new had been set loose within me—a sleeping dog was awakened, but I didn't want to admit it. It didn't take Curt long to say what I'd expected he would: "I think you need to go back to therapy." He and I both knew my reaction had nothing to do with him, and I'd never been afraid of his touch until that moment. I knew in my mind that he was right, but my heart and ego prevented me from wanting to go back to therapy. *There has to be another way,* I told myself. I asked him to let me try one thing first, and I agreed that if that didn't work, I'd go back to therapy.

I had no idea where the odd reaction was coming from. I only knew I didn't want to go back to therapy, so I had to figure it out. I eventually got to the point of not wanting him to touch me, for fear of how I would react, and that was unhealthy for me and for our marriage. Once again, I was afraid. Why does the unknown have to be so scary? I didn't want to deal with any more issues in my life. I thought I was done with the abuse taking its toll on my life, but now I wondered if I'd ever be completely over it. I asked myself, *Will I ever be free of all of it, or will there always be some residue, some dirt left inside me? Can I even be completely cleansed and made whole again?* Thankfully, the fear of the unknown wasn't as great as the fear of a wedge in our marriage.

First, I thought I'd reread a book that had been very helpful to me, *The Sexual Healing Journey*. While Curt was out of town for a weekend, I returned to that book in the hopes that God would lead me to an understanding of what was going on inside and allow me to heal, without the need for additional therapy. I just kept praying that God would bring to light whatever was going on inside of me and that He would help me figure it out without me having to make an appointment. As helpful as therapy had been, I really didn't want to go back. In some way, it felt as if that would be moving backward, and I didn't want to take months to figure it all out.

I reread almost the entire book in grad student-like fashion, just skimming over paragraphs that I felt I already understood. Then I came across a chapter that seemed brand new, as if I were reading it for the first time. I didn't remember reading it the first time. This section addressed the abusive touch actually feeling good to the one being abused. I read about the emotions that come from knowing internally that the touch is bad and inappropriate, yet still being aroused and liking it. Tears began gushing out of me uncontrollably, and I was overcome with a burdensome sense of shame. I saw myself as a two-and-a-half-year-old girl again. I saw the icky neighbor and what he was doing, and I realized that, as a child, I'd actually liked it. *How could I like something so hateful? And how will I ever get over this?* I worried.

That is what happens when we shine a light in a dark corner. All the pain I released made more room for God in my heart. I cried and sobbed for a long time, begging God to free me of the guilt, shame, and confusion. I asked Him to heal my heart and restore my intimacy with Curt. As I prayed, I felt God's comfort. He honored my begging immediately; the shame went away, and the confusion lifted. I knew then that I was going to be okay. I also knew there was one more thing I would need to do for God to complete my healing in that area. I had to tell Curt.

Telling him about the ugly side of the abuse did not get any easier over time, but I took comfort in knowing he had always been supportive and understanding. I knew keeping another secret would only put a crack in our marriage and distance us from each other. I had learned that much, that cracks always become caverns. Keeping my marriage intact was more important to me than hiding the ugly side of me.

When Curt returned home from his weekend away, I told him everything that was going on in my head. It took some time and some self-talk to get the words to come out of my mouth. I told him that I'd reread the book, about my revelation, my tears, my shame, and my prayers. Again, he said it made sense to him. Again, God used Curt to show and teach me about grace and love.

I was relieved but still uneasy, as the power of the shame wasn't gone. I was still nervous about being intimate with Curt. I didn't want to wreck it again. I wanted my husband to have a whole relationship with his wife, the relationship he deserved. I requested that we cross the bridge slowly, and Curt continued to be understanding while God showed me that His light could take away the darkness and replace it with His love.

Fear

We've mentioned fear already, but it can be such a crippling emotion that we should talk a little more about it. Fear can deadlock us. It can completely take us over and paralyze us, leaving us unable to move. That is why cleaning the deep, dark corners is as difficult as it is important. Many of our problems today are rooted in fear, physical as well as emotional. Headaches, ulcers, sleeplessness, panic, lack of trust, and lack of self-confidence are just a few problems that stem from fear. We can fear many things, including rejection and intimacy. Fear hurts all of our relationships and creates a crack that can eventually destroy us and our ability to relate to those around us in a healthy way. The enemy loves to take whatever little piece of darkness we have within us and build on it, and that darkness can only stay tucked away and ignored for so long. After a while, we'll begin to see that the only way to rid ourselves of the darkness is to bring it to the light and let God's love replace it. Every time we look to God and ask the Holy Spirit to replace the darkness with love, we experience victory, both emotional and spiritual. Remember that God doesn't leave a job half-finished. He won't quit, and He wants us completely cleaned.

I was shocked when I read in Dr. Colbert's *Deadly Emotions* that fear triggers more than 1,400 known physical and chemical stress reactions and activates more than 30 different hormones (p.13). No wonder it's associated with so many diseases! Anxiety and over-caring is rooted in the fear of loss. Think about all the situations and people in our lives that raise our anxiety levels. Now think about how many times we revisit those situations. Those physical and chemical reactions happen over and over, yet we wonder why we're so sick so often.

We have to understand that fear has to do with punishment. It cannot produce the wholeness God wants to share with us. For God to transform our hearts to be more like His, He must set a match of His light to our fear and darkness to show us the wonder of living in His love (Jacobsen, p. 79). Responding to God's love will take us much further than fear, as we're told in 1 John 4:18:

> *There is no fear in love. But perfect love drives out fear, because fear has to do with punishment the one who fears is not made perfect in love* (TNIV).

Only God's perfect love can cast out fear; we cannot do it ourselves. Therefore, we need to shine God's light on the areas of fear and release the pain. Yes, it will hurt, but only for a short time. Soon God will fill those dark corners with His love and light.

Have you ever been told, "This is best kept a secret"? That is a lie from the enemy used to keep us in darkness. Dr. Colbert puts it this way:

> Unthinkable childhood traumas can so mar the soul that bitterness and hatred smolder for decades erupting many years later in the form of nightmares, uncontrollable crying, inability to function in daily routines, depression or some other negative behavior (p. 158).

If we live in fear, harboring secrets we don't want anyone else to know, the enemy wins, and we will continue to have struggle after struggle in our relationships, including the one we share with God. It is not worth it.

I don't mean to suggest that this happens in a snap, though it does for some. God revealing Himself to our hearts is usually a process. We have to be willing to invite Him into the process. Every time I tried to do it on my own and control my reactions and emotions, I failed. I had the ungodly belief that I am only safe when I am in control. Choosing to give up control actually meant living without fear. For me, it was a process of turning on the light.

Dealing with fear is, perhaps, the most difficult part of cleaning behind the fridge. It keeps us from even beginning to clean those dark corners. We have left it untouched for years for a reason—it's painful! Once we have tackled the fear, though, we can turn on the light, and that will change everything.

Chapter 5

Cleaning Behind the Fridge:
Light burns away the darkness

Cleaning behind the fridge requires a willingness to become vulnerable and face the areas of our lives that hold us back from being everything God has created us to be. Walking away from fear and purposefully into light requires a lot of trust. The One we really need to trust is God; we can rely on His unconditional love and grace, and His light removes the fear, pain, and sense of unworthiness.

Turning on the Light

So what do we do to move out of fear and darkness? We turn on the light, God's light, so He can burn away the darkness. If we return to 1 John 1:5b-7, we'll read,

God is light; in Him there is no darkness at all. If we claim to have fellowship with Him and yet walk in the darkness, we lie and do not live out the truth. But if we walk in the light, as He is in the light, we have fellowship with one another, and the blood of Jesus, His Son, purifies us from all sin (TNIV).

If we choose God's light, there is no darkness. We will

have fellowship with Him, and the blood of Jesus will cleanse us of sin. Cleansing and forgiving of sins are really two different things. There are things I have asked God to forgive me for over and over. Yes, He forgives us the first time we ask, but the shame and guilt can remain. I still carried the defilement around with me, and I began to build thought habits, lies that the enemy used to keep me from God. When God turns on the light, that means He's actively cleaning house—cleansing and not just forgiving.

Choosing light allows us to stop making excuses, stop blaming ourselves and others, and accept responsibility for our reactions to what God is showing us. Here is what I mean: When I was watching that movie with Curt and a little switch went off, I believe God was trying to reveal to me an area of darkness that He wanted to cleanse. I could have chosen to push it back down within myself, back under the cover of darkness, like so many of us often do. However, that would have meant living a lie that would separate me from God, from the love and intimacy He desires with all His children.

After making the choice to let Him continue to reveal to me what had been hidden, I had to tell Curt. *The Calvary Road* author Roy Hession says, "While we are in that condition of darkness, we cannot have true fellowship with our brother [sister] either, for we are not real with them" (p. 33). I had to be real with Curt to build intimacy with him and with God.

For the cycle of healing to be complete, we must have someone in our lives with whom we can share the deepest and darkest. Because our relationship with our family and friends and God are so linked, we cannot disturb one without disturbing the other (Hession, p. 46). That person must be someone who makes us feel safe. For those who are married, the spouse should be that person. Clearly, Curt is my safe place. However, if there is a history of violence in any relationship, it isn't safe to share the deepest, darkest secrets with the violent one or the abuser, regardless of who they are. For those who do not have a safe relationship with someone who is mature in Christ, it is best to seek the help of a trained and trusted counselor or pastor to begin bringing those difficult issues to light.

As I have said, I really believe secrets between spouses start as cracks and end up as caverns. I would have felt guilty for keeping a secret, and guilt tends to grow and fester; eventually, it would have only pushed us further apart, and I couldn't let that happen.

I have started to see that there is a relationship between the level of intimacy we have with our spouses and other significant relationships and the level of intimacy we have with God. I believe if I am holding back from my relationship with my husband by harboring secrets and not dealing with issues that stem from the abuse, I will not be able to let God fully into my life, nor will I follow His will for my life. If I am not able to fully express my love for my husband, I don't think I can fully express to God my love for Him or receive the fullness of His love for me. We all need someone we can be completely raw and honest with and still be loved. I have always known in my head that God loves me, warts and all; however, my heart didn't experience it until I told Curt. Not only did my relationship with Curt deepen, but so did my relationship with God.

God couldn't provide true healing without me telling

Curt each time an issue arose. My relationship with Curt was not the only thing at stake. Had I not released those secrets, darkness would have lurked in my life; secrets produce darkness, and that darkness gives the enemy opportunity to work. He will use that opportunity to produce more and more darkness. At that time, I had no idea that God was protecting me from the enemy. All I saw was increased intimacy in my relationship with Curt. Obviously that was good, but it was just the beginning of the work God wanted to do in me. What I understand now is that God wants His light to shine in all the areas of our lives. Only then is there no place for the enemy to be. Only then can we be completely clean. We can take some encouragement from Romans 13:12:

> *The night is nearly over; the day is almost here. So let us put aside the deeds of darkness and put on the armor of light.*

God will show us where to begin if we ask and if we are obedient to what He shows us. He will replace our darkness to overflowing with His Holy Spirit (Hession, p. 27). That is the first step in cleaning behind the fridge: letting God shine His light wherever He wants to begin cleaning. Yuck has been growing back there for years, so it's best to let Him show you where to start.

Of course there is another side to this. We also have to be willing to receive light from others. I would have no doubt put off dealing with what God was trying to reveal if Curt hadn't said I should go back to therapy. I had to be willing to receive those words from him. It hurt not because of what he said, but because my heart knew he was right. God uses others to hold a light up for us to see. It says in 2 Corinthians

4:2, "We are to renounce secret and shameful ways and we commend ourselves to everyone's conscience in the sight of God" (TNIV). We have to put our pride aside and receive. It is the refusal to die to the self that makes one miserable (Hession, p. 26).

It is so easy to get trapped by darkness. Who really wants to expose their innermost thoughts and beliefs about themselves? It is painful to make ourselves vulnerable. You might ask, "Is it really worth it?" My answer to that question is a resounding, "Yes! Yes! Yes!" I had no idea my heart could feel love like this and that my life could be so unburdened. Choosing light always relieves the pain and lifts the burden: "For you were once darkness, but now you are light in the Lord. Live as children of the light" (Ephesians 5:8). What I know now is that I had a broken heart. My soul needed to be nourished by God's light and love, not my conscience fixed. Things still come up that are painful and burdensome, but I know God will bring me the light I need to clean it up.

What I Am Just Beginning to Understand

Before I had a full understanding of light, I had to learn more about darkness. Satan has dominion over darkness, and he was trying to keep me there, locked in it, so I couldn't fulfill the purposes God had for me. He can introduce thoughts and try to coerce us to live independently of God (*Bondage Breakers*, p. 58). The good news is that since we are with Christ in the light, we don't have to live in the shadows. It is our responsibility to choose truth and resist the devil (p. 27). We all have authority over Satan because of our position in Christ, but we need to know how to exercise that authority.

Rereading the journal I'd written while in therapy, I found

an entry about a dream I had. At the time, the dream freaked me out, but now I can look back on it in a new light. In that dream, Heidi, my friend and boss at the time, looked at me, and an unseen individual said I looked possessed when a spirit whirled my hair and left my body. I wondered, *Was I fighting a demon? Was the Holy Spirit casting out something on my behalf? Was God trying to show me that He was freeing me of something?* I didn't see it that way then, but now, as I've learned more about spiritual warfare, I think it was a real demon in my dream.

When I told the devil to get out after that terrible vision, I believe the Holy Spirit was acting on my behalf. At that time in my life, I didn't have much experience or understanding of demons. Quite frankly, I didn't pay attention to them or anything about them. It never occurred to me that the enemy would be actively working against me everyday. The church I was raised in didn't teach about demons, so it wasn't until I began working in my current church that my eyes were opened to that area of scripture and life with Christ. Matthew 16:18 says,

> I will give you the keys of the kingdom of Heaven; whatever you bind on Earth will be bound in Heaven, and whatever you loose on Earth will be loosed in Heaven (TNIV).

It was a relief to finally understand what the experience meant. I began to have more experiences of demons in my dreams, but I knew how to bind them and cast them out. I still have to remind myself that Satan is the father of lies and disguises himself as an angel of light (2 Corinthians 11:14).

This is not about crying, "It's the devil!" in every circumstance. Rather, it is about acknowledging that there is a spiritual realm at work in our lives, along with free will. The enemy will take subtle and obvious measures to keep us from the love of God, and the enemy wants to prevent us from sharing God's love with others. It is easy to focus on the negative; the more I obsessed over that fleeting thought, the more room there was for the enemy to pull me away from God. As soon as I was obedient to the nudge of God, I received the blessing of His peace and comfort. Sometimes we need to cast out demons, but mostly we need to be obedient to God's will for our lives. In his article, "No Fear," Jack Frost puts it like this:

> We either live our life as if we have a home, or we live our life as if we don't have a home. We either live our life feeling safe and secure and at rest in Father's heart, living to experience His love and give it away, or we live our live in fear and uncertainty, struggling constantly with the fear of rejection and the fear of opening up our heart to love.

The more I have become aware of the times in my life when the enemy has tried to come against me, the more I've learned to rely on God and His understanding rather than my own. Giving myself to Him and submitting to His will versus my own has been really difficult, but it's a great relief to know I am not in charge.

I encourage you to look at your life and experiences in this perspective. Could it be the enemy is trying to prevent us from running into God's arms? Has God been nudging us? Are we struggling to follow His call? Is it worth it to the enemy to get in the way? Yes! Remember that God has a plan

51

for us, and even if we cannot see it right now, He wants us to prosper. Jeremiah 29:11 says,

"For I know the plans I have for you," declares the Lord, "plans to prosper you and not to harm you, plans to give you hope and a future."

Beyond fear and darkness and the enemy himself, there is something else that gets in the way of experiencing the fullness of God's love: ourselves.

Forgiving Yourself

It may sound easy, but frankly, I think forgiving myself is one of the hardest things I've ever had to do. Honestly, this is an area I am still working on, and it has been a slow, tedious process that has uncovered a layer of grime and pain I had no idea existed behind my fridge. Many of the books I've read gloss over this concept; they all seem to say, "Just do it," as if it's as simple as putting on a pair of Nike shoes. If only it were that easy! In fact, it has turned into one of the most complex concepts I have tried to understand. It has been easier to forgive my molester than to forgive myself for participating in the act, for not being a perfect parent, for having a son born with heart disease, and for not protecting my son on the school bus. I am much harder on myself than I am on others. Sure, I managed to let go of little pieces here and there, but it took years to completely let go. God did a real number on my heart for me to finally get it, and I'm so thankful He's not a quitter!

An unwillingness to forgive myself meant I was choosing to continue to live in a cycle of pain and darkness. I struggled with forgiving myself for not protecting my son. I had to stop telling myself I was unworthy of forgiveness. I kept declaring to myself, "I am not worth God's love, blessings, and the gift of His Son." That had to change. Holding on to pain and self-disgust was a sin that prevented me from fully trusting God and accepting His love, a love that does not judge (Jacobson, p. 128). It wasn't easy for me to let go of my own despair and trust God's unconditional love.

I kept insisting that I couldn't possibly forgive myself. I really didn't know how to let go. In an effort to change my internal tapes, I started saying, "Yes, I will forgive myself." Of course, that begged the question of when. I could have spent the rest of my life saying I would and never following through with it. Finally, one night while praying, I heard God say, "Not 'I will'...but 'I do!' Repeat it." It was such a simple statement, but a true one. At that point, I began telling myself, "I do forgive you." It was a good beginning for me, but it was only that—a beginning.

Then I felt God nudging me to read Isaiah 53, a painfully vivid prophecy of Christ's crucifixion and death. I was reminded as I read it of the lengths God went to in order to declare us forgiven. Not forgiving myself was rooted in a feeling of unworthiness, and that became a barrier in accepting God's love. God was telling me, "You are worthy," and Isaiah 53 describes just how worthy. How could I accept His forgiveness and not forgive myself? That was what Isaiah 53 really said to me. If I were going to accept God's forgiveness of me, I had to forgive myself, because my sin was washed away. By saying "I *will* forgive myself" rather than "I *do* forgive myself," I was not accepting God's forgiveness. Could it be that simple? It certainly didn't feel that way.

I was getting closer, but I knew I hadn't fully let go, even though I really wanted to. One thing I needed to forgive myself for was not being a perfect parent. I hadn't lived up to my own expectations of parenting, and I was burdened by it. My son had been emotionally hurt by a bully on the bus, and I was unable to protect him as I thought I should have been able to. I internalized the thought that it was my fault he'd been hurt, something many parents probably go through.

I am slowly learning that God doesn't bring healing cognitively; rather, he brings it through the heart. Just understanding that I needed to forgive myself wasn't doing it. I needed to transfer that knowing from my head to my heart, which required direct intervention by God. First, I had a dream. In that dream, my husband had an affair. I was supposed to forgive him, but I couldn't let go of the disgust. As I wrote that in my journal, it became clear to me that it was not about my marriage. People we know in our dreams usually represent something in ourselves (Virlker, *Hearing the Voice of God*). Curt was me in that dream; in other words, I was supposed to forgive myself, but I couldn't let go of the disgust. Realizing that I was still disgusted with me, not with him was a major aha moment.

As I continued to pray and journal, I felt an overwhelming sense of the Holy Spirit come over me. Then I heard, "You need to let it go. You are not responsible."

I responded, "How? I don't know what to do differently. I feel so...guilty."

I heard, "No! I'm guilty! I'm responsible! I chose not to intervene! I chose to let it happen. It is about healing. My love is bigger than all of this."

I responded, "But I'm his mother."

I heard, "You are his earthly parent. I am his Father!"

It was quite the kick in the gut, but it was so true. After crying a mountain of tears, it finally moved out of my head and into my heart, and I finally let go. The sense of disgust was finally gone.

Unlike forgiving others, forgiving yourself results in a cleansing of shame, pain, and disgust. Forgiving myself means trusting that God's love is greater than my sin. Greater trust means I let God further into my heart. It has been and continues to be a long, painful process but a rewarding one. The more I let go of myself and turn over my heart to God, the more love I am able to receive from Him, and the more I am able to live out of joy and love rather than pain and brokenness. Forgiving myself has meant I am able to more fully surrender to Him. I wish I could say I am 100 percent there, but we all know that won't happen in this life. I have forgiven myself for the toughest stuff so far, but living means more wounding. Hopefully forgiving myself won't be so hard in the future.

Worthiness

So many times, I've heard that we don't deserve God's grace and love. I have even said it myself. I've always felt unworthy of God's grace and have always struggled with those kinds of statements. I agree there is nothing we can say or do to make God love us any more or less than He does; that is grace. What I struggle with is feeling as if I don't deserve it.

Worthiness takes its roots in being commendable, excellent, and honorable, one who is deserving is someone who is worthy or suitable for reward. So often I hear Christians say we are unworthy or don't deserve God's love. Many suggest that because we are born of sin, we are inherently bad, but I beg to differ. We are created in God's image. By His own admission, what He created is good (Genesis 1). Over and over again in scripture, God chooses His children. He goes after the least likely and shows them how great His love is for them. Consider Moses, David, and Paul. Were they worthy? By the world's standards, and even by the Church's, probably not, but God saw in them what He'd originally created in them: His image and His heart. Why would God go to such great lengths to express His love for us if we are unworthy? He doesn't. He created us as beings worthy of His love and a relationship with Him.

My feelings of unworthiness came from this world, not from God. It was an ungodly belief that prevented me from moving God's love from my head to my heart. God loves us so much that He sent His Son, and that Son, Jesus, said He was going to his Father's house to prepare a place for us (John 14:2). Would He do that if we were unworthy? I needed to move out of that cycle and allow myself to accept the fullness of God's love for me. Once I allowed my heart to feel and trust His love, my heart really began to change.

In his book, *From Spiritual Slavery to Spiritual Sonship*, Jack Frost describes it as an "orphan heart," one that feels it does not have a safe, secure place in a father's heart to be loved, valued, and affirmed (p. 43). Once I felt safe in God's love, I felt worthy of all the love God has for me. It's knowing that God loves me as His creation, not what I do to deserve His love (p. 46). I used to think God keeps a daily to-do list for me, things I have to accomplish each day to be good in His eyes. That is orphan thinking, and it's a lie I'd bought into, but we'll talk more on that later. For now, it can be said that having turned on the light to the depth of His love for all of His children has freed me from the bondage of feeling unworthy.

Conclusion

There were many lessons for me to learn while cleaning behind the fridge, and it was an exhausting process. I do feel freed from burdens I wasn't even aware I was carrying in my heart. I learned the value of letting go of pride and humbling my heart in the name of His love and for the sake of my relationships with Him and with others.

Each time I shined God's light on dark places, there was revelation, often coupled with pain. The hardest part about shining His light on dark places is that for His love to come in, the pain has to go out. That means feeling the pain all over again; hence, the motivation for all those tears I shed. The beauty is that once you've done that, the darkness is replaced with love and light. We don't have to carry the darkness and pain around anymore. The empty feeling in the corner of my heart is now full of God's love. As hard as it was to pull out the fridge and shine light on all that yuck, the reward is forever life-changing, and I wouldn't trade it for anything. Thank You, God, for letting Your love and light shine into my dark places.

Chapter 6

Dusting the Furniture:
Essentials stand clear

The heavy-duty cleaning was done. I'd dug into those messy closets, reorganized, and thrown junk out. I'd gotten into those icky, dark corners and attacked with bleach. I felt pretty good, and the house was starting to look nice, but I looked around and saw a thin layer of dust covering the furniture. It was not a tough job, just one more thing to do. I was feeling tired and not up to one more thing, but I wanted everything to sparkle and shine like new. I knew I could do it, so I grabbed that rag and polished, deciding I wanted to get the job completely done.

Much to my surprise, the house sparkled when I was finished, and I had no idea cleaning house could feel so good! When I started, the task was huge and overwhelming. I can't believe I considered leaving the job undone. I realize now that all the hard work was worth it, in far greater ways than I ever expected. Now I can sit back, relax, and enjoy a job well done, at least for a little while.

This is why we mustn't neglect polishing the furniture. We could ignore this task, as it wouldn't be the end of the world, but that would be like leaving the icing off the cake. It makes the entire house so much cleaner, more pristine, welcoming, and comfortable. I waited years to polish the furniture, and frankly, I didn't even realize I could do it. I didn't know it could be so shiny and sparkling new. In some areas, the dust was a little thicker than I anticipated, but taking care of the little things left me feeling even closer to God than I expected. It might take a little elbow grease, but the scripture assures us that He won't quit until the essentials stand clear. He will take us that far if we're willing to go there with Him.

I didn't know God's healing could be so complete that I could feel like a new creation. The memories are still there, but they don't affect me the same way anymore. They don't affect my relationship with my husband or my kids. I now feel pure love in my heart, rather than just knowing it in my head. If you haven't started dusting and polishing yet, you should, for pure joy awaits. Remember that dusting can be done more than once; it's never good to let the dust build up too thick. We can learn new things each time we dust, so grab that rag or Swiffer, and let's get dusting!

I Am Free

Shortly after God instructed me to write this book, I contacted Chuck Ripka, a friend and the author of a book I'd just finished reading, *God Out of the Box*. I was eager to talk with Chuck about my new adventure. He suggested that what I needed was to go through a "generational healing" and mentioned that his brother-in-law, Richard Sicheneder, was just the person to facilitate it. I had no idea what it meant or entailed, as it wasn't part of the teachings I'd grown up with or learned about as an adult. It was, in essence, way outside my United Methodist box, but I knew if Chuck suggested it, it had to be okay. I was certain I'd learn something and that the Holy Spirit would be present, and if Chuck's hunch was right, I would want my entire family to go through it.

I contacted Richard and arranged the prayer meeting. There were three on the prayer team that day: Richard, Chuck, and a woman. Richard started by giving me a scriptural understanding of why we need to undergo such healings. He used scriptures from the Old and New Testaments, and in some cases, we went back to the original Hebrew for a better understanding of current translations. It was a lot to absorb in one meeting, but it all made sense, and it quickly became clear to me that there were generational attachments affecting my life. I was ready for that to end.

We began praying, and I repented for myself and my ancestors, then broke the ties that bound these spirits to myself and would bind them to future generations. Richard helped me with the praying by saying the prayers and allowing me to repeat them. We covered a lot of territory, from hard-heartedness to victim and harlot spirit, and on and on. Still, as much as I enjoyed it and learned from it, it was difficult to believe those recited prayers would make any real difference in my life.

Chuck stood in representation for the men in my life and repented for all the wrongdoings they had done. Specifically, he stood in for my father and repented for Dad's inability to protect me from the abuse I suffered. I can't describe how powerful it was to hear those words. I have never blamed my parents, so it never occurred to me that I might be holding on to that hidden pain or resentment. Before I knew it, I was sobbing, with tears running down my face. The pain was being released and replaced with God's love for me, and I found that overwhelming. We also asked the Holy Spirit to restore my body and mind to its original state. I had no idea I had so much garbage to pray through.

Before we finished, they offered to fill me with the Holy Spirit. Not knowing what that meant, I still agreed. I had heard of other people being "slain" in the Spirit, and I understood it from a biblical perspective. I'd even witnessed it in the past, though it wasn't something the church I grew up in talked about or practiced. I had felt the presence of the Holy Spirit before, but this was much greater. It was, for lack of a better word, amazing. They kept saying, "Fill her, Lord. Fill her, Lord," and as I stood in the middle of the room, I thought I was going to lift off the ground. I felt light as a feather, and all I could see was a bright white light. For the first time, I actually physically felt God's love for me. I had known it intellectually, but that was the first time I felt it in my heart, which He'd been changing all along. My burdens were lifted, and my heart was more open to love than ever before. It truly went beyond feeling God's love for me; it was fuller and more profound than anything I'd experienced before. It was pure joy, and God's love became real to me in a whole new way.

When I left, I was exhausted, emotionally, physically, and spiritually. I had cried a pool of tears, but I didn't notice the fullness of what had happened in me until later. I had changed in ways I didn't expect. I had changed in ways I didn't even know were possible. It started with the first time Curt and I were intimate after that, an interlude that ended very tearfully for me. Curt, concerned, asked what was wrong. I assured him they were tears of joy, and he was dumbfounded. For the first time, I didn't feel dirty in the least bit. I had grown so used to the feeling of residue that I'd stopped noticing it was even there until it was gone, and I cried in amazement. God had washed me clean as snow. I had never known anyone could feel like that; I'd always assumed everyone felt a little dirty, a little dusty. Not everyone feels that way though. I know that now because I don't feel like that anymore. It's a kind of freedom I struggle to describe. I just want everyone who has been victimized to know that you can feel clean again, and every ounce of residue can be purged from your life by God.

I now feel a deeper love than I've ever felt before for Curt and my boys. Even better, just as there is nothing in the way of my expression of love to my family, there is nothing in the way of me experiencing my heavenly Father's love. Previously there were always thin walls between me and others, between me and God, but I didn't realize those were there either—not until they were gone. It was a very subtle yet profound change, and it affected the way I'd interact with others from then on. My level of compassion for others deepened greatly.

The other major difference I noticed within the first week was that I no longer felt rage. Before the healing, my anger would quickly burn hot, until I felt completely out of control. I would shake on the inside, and it often terrified me as I was afraid of what I might do while in that state. It was one of the reasons that Curt and I decided against spanking our children. Curt had always told me that his anger never felt out of control, and I didn't believe him. I was sure everyone felt the way I did at times. I was sure everyone felt rage now and then.

I first recognized this change when, after a worship service on a Sunday morning, my son had a complete and total meltdown. Previously, I would have started seething on the inside, and my heart would have raced. The more defiant he would become, the more I would shake on the inside. This time, though, about a week after my time with Richard and Chuck, I was calm. I just picked my child up and carried him to the car, all while he was kicking and screaming. I didn't even feel angry, and I couldn't believe my own calm reaction. Of course I get angry from time to time now, but there is absolutely no rage. Now I believe my husband: I know it's possible to be angry without feeling out-of-control rage.

Sexual abuse and rage were some things that had been passed down our family line, and I knew those affected me. I'm sure there were other generational issues I was not aware of as well. Closing generational doors and breaking ungodly soul ties were areas of scripture and prayer I had never given much thought to, and I had little understanding of them. I'd always thought that I was automatically a new creature just by believing in Christ, that it was all that was required in regard to the enemy, but it's not that simple. The experience was so profound that I wanted my entire family to experience it. A couple months later, I took two of my sisters to a corporate healing session. Several months after that, we brought Richard and his team to my hometown to facilitate a corporate healing for my entire family, forty-five of us in all. After that, God began restoring our family in ways we never expected; it closed doors we thought were just a part of life, then opened doors that drew us closer to Him.

Generational Teaching

I want to outline for you a brief description of the teaching Richard provides so you can begin to understand, just to wet your appetite. I encourage everyone to go through a formal teaching and prayer time, and I guarantee that if you do, you won't be the same.

When we take a look at our family history, we may dig up some things we'd rather not see: anger, abuse, heart disease, or alcoholism, for example. That was the easiest way for me to see issues that have been handed down for generations. We often deal with problems at the surface. We might just stop drinking, but the desire remains. We try to just stop hitting, but the desire is still there. We have pruned the bad behaviors, but we haven't dealt with the root of the problem. If there is a disease in our garden, do we just prune back the vine to get rid of the disease, or do we treat the roots to change the plant from within? We have to treat the roots of our family trees to change our lives and the lives of our children and grandchildren.

There are two other words in the Bible for sin: transgression and iniquity. Exodus 34:5-9 says,

Now the Lord descended in the cloud and stood with him there, and proclaimed the name of the Lord. And the Lord passed before him and proclaimed, "The Lord, the Lord God, merciful and gracious, longsuffering, and abounding in goodness and truth keeping mercy for thousands, forgiving iniquity and transgression and sin, by no means clearing the guilty, visiting the iniquity of the fathers upon the children and the children's children to the third and fourth generation."

So Moses made haste and bowed his head toward the Earth and worshiped. The he said, "If now I have found grace in Your sight, O Lord, let my Lord, I pray, go among

us, even though we are stiff-necked people and pardon our iniquity and our sin and take us as Your inheritance" (NKJV).

To break this down, sin is an offense; it is missing the mark, goal, or path. Transgression is rebellion; it means to choose to be misguided or to break away from authority. Lastly, iniquity is perversity, depravity, a condition of guilt, a consequence of sin. It means to be bent, twisted, or perverted. You might be wondering, "So what?" While I was growing up, I'd often heard of sin and transgressions in warnings of things I shouldn't do. I knew to repent for my sins if I'd done wrong or had offended someone, but I'd never really heard of iniquity. It is used less and less in various translations of the Bible, and it appears as unrighteousness and wickedness in some places. Iniquity is God's way of giving each generation a chance to right the wrongs of their forefathers. He gives each generation a new chance to allow Him to be the full source of love and grace in their lives. He wants to cleanse us and completely restore us into the persons He created us to be. Satan is given authority to traffic in areas were sin has opened the door. If we don't close the door, it remains open for our children and their children. In other words, the iniquity is passed on to the next generation in the hopes that we will repent for the wrong of the past and fall fully into God's embrace. God has power over Satan through the cross, but authority is given to Satan through sin. As Dutch Sheets puts it, "Where God and Satan are concerned, the issue has never been power; it is always and only a question of authority" (*Authority in Prayer*, p. 20). This generational teaching is mentioned within the New Testament as well.

Look at 2 Timothy 2:19-21:

Nevertheless the solid foundation of God stands, having this seal: "The Lord knows those who are His," and, "Let everyone who names the name of Christ depart from iniquity." But in a great house, there are not only vessels of gold and silver, but also of wood and clay, some for honor and some for dishonor. Therefore, if anyone cleanses himself from the latter, he will be a vessel for honor, sanctified and useful for the Master, prepared for every good work (NKJV).

This is not about our eternity with God in heaven. It is about right here, right now. It is about our lives being a true reflection of our God of grace and love. The enemy is of this world and has been given the right to interfere in our lives where there is an open door. But this is not about using the devil as an excuse and crying, "The devil made me do it!" around every corner. It is about resting in the arms of our Creator every day, calling upon Him to fight the spiritual battles, about being blatantly honest with God and allowing Him into every corner of our hearts.

Victim Spirit

Let's look more closely at one spiritual attachment and mindset that is common to those who have been abused, so we can see how these attachments play out in a person's life. "Victim spirit" is used rather loosely to describe a kind of demonic attachment, as well as a mindset that a person can have.

Have you ever looked at someone and thought they seemed to have a flashing beacon over their head that brought bad stuff their way? Do you know people who have left one abusive relationship only to enter another one? A victim spirit will attract predator spirits, and it persuades the person that there is nothing they can do to change their situation. Have you ever gone to work with someone on a project and found yourself completely retreating into the background? Do you just let others take over? Do you feel like bad things always happen to you? It could be that there's much at work than bad luck.

> Once the demonic attachment is broken, it is impor-
> tant to continue to work on changing the mindset so
> that we don't fall back into old habits that might open
> the door to sin. This will not feel natural, even after
> the attachment is broken. A person trying to move
> past this must continue to walk in truth, even though
> it doesn't feel right. Even if we've faced a continuous
> string of problems in the past, the future does not
> have to be the same. Patterns can change, and re-
> signed hopelessness is not one of the fruits of the
> spirit. (Taken from *Overcoming the Victim Spirit*—A
> Plumbline Ministries book).

Once the demonic attachment is gone and one confronts a predator demon, the demon retreats. We need to walk in the authority given to us through Christ. Once we recognize a demonic attachment, we must bind it verbally in the name of Jesus Christ, Son of God. We must command it to leave and never return again, then invite the Holy Spirit to fill the areas that were vacated.

Here's the good news: We are called to walk in dominion over darkness, and all we have to do is evict it. Dominion is the extreme opposite of victimization. It is life-giving. It is not domination or force; dominion builds up and does not tear down. It is part of our inheritance as children of God (*Overcoming the Victim Spirit*).

This is an art. As we begin to walk in freedom and truth, we will see others differently. We have new tools of discernment when we meet an offensive person. We can ask, "Are they rude, wounded, or walking with an attachment?" God will show us what we are dealing with as we walk in dominion.

I noticed that the victim spirit was gone when I no longer took everything personally. Prior to that, if anyone criticized a project I was working on, I'd internalize it as being a failure. If there were some family drama going on, I would get wrapped up in it, as if it were happening to me; I couldn't keep an objective distance. After the generational healing and removal of the victim spirit, I was shocked to find that I wasn't internalizing criticism and was able to keep an appropriate distance from family drama. Every once in a while, I catch myself wanting to buy into one of the enemy's lies. I know it's not of God, though, so I bind it and cast it out. The freedom I've achieved from the generational healing has shown up in so many areas of my life. I have a new sense of joy and freedom, and I now have a sense of what God means when He says He wants to do a thorough housecleaning and leave only the essentials.

Chapter 7

Dusting the Furniture:
Essentials I discovered

The generational experience was a great way for me to dust the furniture. It opened the door for me to learn more about some of the essentials of living as the person God created me to be. These essentials are part of my daily life as I continue to work with Him in the refining process.

Repentance

During the generational healing, I spent a lot of time repenting. Repentance encompasses more than asking God for forgiveness of our sins. Repentance includes cleansing. Growing up, I was told repentance meant asking for forgiveness, that the two concepts were one and the same. It was actually freeing to learn that it was so much more than that. I love the way Dan Allender puts it in *The Wounded Heart*: "Repentance is to move from rebellion and denial to truth and surrender" (p. 197). It is taking off our masks and allowing ourselves to be seen in full light by God. Thomas Merton once said, "Sin is giving God a mask when God is looking for a face."

First John 1:9 scripture reminds us that forgiveness of sin

and cleansing of sin are two separate things, and repentance includes both. "If we confess our sins, He is faithful and righteous to forgive us our sins and to cleanse us from all unrighteousness" (NASB).

Martin Luther defined repentance (*metanoia* in Greek) as signifying a change of the mind and heart, something similar to metamorphosis. The manner for changing it is the grace of God (metanoiaministries.com).

As a victim, I had to remember that it was not about past abuse. I didn't need to repent for being abused. It was about my reaction to the abuse. I had built a wall of self-protection around myself, and that wall made it difficult for me to trust others or God. I was going to be in control of my life. Nobody was going to tell me what to do or how to do it, not even God. When I realized that I had that wall around me, preventing me from allowing God fully into my life, I knew I had some repenting to do. I was broken, humbled, and ready to change.

In an amazing little book, *The Calvary Road*, Roy Hession talks about the choice to become broken and repent or remain in the self:

> It is always the self who gets irritable and envious and resentful and critical and worried. It is the self who is hard and unyielding in its attitudes toward others. It is the self who is shy and self-conscious and reserved. Then we can stiffen our necks and refuse to repent, or we can bow the head and say, "Yes, Lord."

It was pretty easy for me to see myself in that description. There is no doubt that repentance is hard, humbling, and brings me to my knees. Hession goes on to say that at no point should we protest our innocence of what God shows us. Oh boy, I certainly have not enjoyed all the things God has shown me. I remind myself that it is only when I am broken that He can change my heart. This scripture has been a helpful reminder of why we repent.

Ezekiel 18:30 tells us,

Therefore, O house of Israel, I will judge you, each one according to his ways, declares the Sovereign Lord. Repent! Turn away from all your offenses; then sin will not be your downfall.

The change that comes from repentance allows us to walk more closely with God and allows us to produce fruit for Him as it says in Matthew 3:8: "Therefore, bear fruit in keeping with repentance" (NASB).

True repentance is about relationship, and it will help restore, expand, and grow our relationships with God and others. Let me try to explain. In a meeting at church, I made a statement that the pastor and two others took in a completely different light than I intended. The pastor brought it to my attention, and I realized how my words had been misunderstood.

I had two choices. I could take the information and go on my way and do nothing; but if I did that, I didn't know what might happen when I came into contact with those same people in the future. I would most likely put on a mask and pretend I hadn't offended them and that our relationship was the same as it had always been. That would have resulted in a wall going up between us, one I was sure they would sense; every time they saw me, they'd be reminded of what I'd said, and our relationship would be clouded. Time would pass, and the wall wouldn't stick out as much, but it would remain until I dealt with it. The same is true with our relationship with God. I would have put up a wall between God and myself as well.

The second choice was to deal with what I had said, and that was what I chose to do. It definitely stung to go to friends and apologize for the misunderstanding, and I even choked up; but when it was over, my relationships were restored, and I was cleansed. I believe the apology built trust between us and strengthened the relationships rather than destroying them the way silence would have.

With true repentance, our heart changes, and our walls continue to come down. Then we're able to see others with new eyes. Sometimes this allows us to see our role in a broken relationship with new eyes. Part of repentance can include going to others for forgiveness.

We should ask for God's forgiveness, but we may also need to seek it from others, such as our parents or authority figures. This is sometimes referred to as "the ministry of restitution." A block may exist in the relationship until we acknowledge that we have wronged someone, intentionally or not, just as in the example above.

Even though God forgives us the first time we ask, we may continue to reap what we have sown until we restore the broken relationship, as indicated in Matthew 21-26:

> *You're familiar with the command to the ancients, "Do not murder." I'm telling you that anyone who is so much as angry with a brother or sister is guilty of murder. Carelessly call a brother "Idiot!" and you just might find yourself hauled into court. Thoughtlessly yell "Stupid!" at a*

sister, and you are on the brink of hellfire. The simple moral fact is that words kill. This is how I want you to conduct yourself in these matters. If you enter your place of worship and, about to make an offering, you suddenly remember a grudge a friend has against you, abandon your offering, leave immediately, go to this friend, and make things right. Then and only then, come back and work things out with God.2 Or say you're out on the street and an old enemy accosts you. Don't lose a minute. Make the first move; make things right with him. After all, if you leave the first move to him, knowing his track record, you're likely to end up in court, maybe even jail. If that happens, you won't get out without a stiff fine (MSG).

When relationships are broken and we are at fault, we mustn't build walls. We need to make the first move to restore that relationship, and repentance is the restoration we need.

Submission

Another area of dusting that I never paid attention to is submission. I didn't pay attention to it because I thought it was equal to oppression. Apparently God had a few things to show me in this area as well. Submission has always been a dirty word to me, a suggestion that someone else had control of me. I felt strongly that women shouldn't be controlled by their husbands, and as a self-reliant, independent woman, submission was completely unacceptable. I really believed no one would or should have control of me. I certainly wasn't going to be some meek, quiet mom who never questioned the orders of her husband. Marriage was to be a partnership; otherwise, I'd have no part of it.

Today, I have a very different view of submission and what it means to be subject to something or someone. Submission is about a relationship and supporting that relationship. Much of my new understanding comes from Jack Frost's teaching in *Spiritual Slavery to Spiritual Sonship*.

The reality is that I am not in control of my life. In fact, none of us really are. God is, and if we are not subject to God's mission, we will be subject to the enemy's. In Greek, submission means to get underneath or be dependent. God calls us to be in submission to others if we are going to be in submission to Him. I began to understand how this is lived out in relationships even before I tagged it with the label of submission.

For several years, I'd been volunteering with an organization called Youth Specialties at their National Youthworkers Convention. This served as my continuing education for youth ministry and made it affordable for me to attend. After ten-plus years of volunteering with the same people, it had become as much a family reunion as it was continuing education. It was always a time of spiritual renewal as well. Needless to say, this was the one thing I looked forward to each year.

One particular year, my husband was at home with two small children to care for while working, and he caught the flu. This began to take its toll on Curt, and he called me while I was away to express his distress. He also said it would be my last year volunteering so I should make the most of it. I was instantly enraged. *Who does he think he is, telling me I have to give up this trip?* I had enough sense to know that trying to solve the issue over the phone was pointless, so we decided to finish the conversation when I returned home.

I hung up the phone and sobbed, then played out my entire side of the argument in my head. It sounded a little like this: *If I have to give this up, what will you give up? Fishing opener? Hunting? This is the only thing I do for me that takes me away from home. How can you be so selfish? Don't you know how much I sacrifice for you all year long?* This went on for quite a while.

Finally in an effort to calm myself down, I jumped in the shower. Then it hit me like a brick: To whom am I going to be subject? The enemy doesn't get my marriage! It became glaringly apparent to me that this disagreement could put a huge wedge of resentment in our marriage. Thankfully God stopped me and showed me what I was doing wrong, and mind you, it was not really a pleasant experience. God showed me that I was about to damage my relationship with Curt over a trip. It really was about our relationship, not about me getting my way.

When I returned home, Curt and I sat down to talk it out. In his mind, we probably could have waited until the following year to make a decision about the following year's trip. I hashed it over in my mind, and I couldn't let it go until we talked about it. He listened as I shared with him what the trip meant to me. I told him that it was more than continuing education, that it was about renewal and reunion. I shared with him that I appreciated the sacrifices he'd made in order for me to take this trip. I also told him that if the trip required too much of a sacrifice for him, I would not ask to go again. He had to know that our marriage meant more to me than the trip. Curt responded by saying he'd had a very difficult week being sick, but he couldn't possibly ask me to give up the trip.

At that time, I only knew I was protecting my marriage. Now I see it as an act of submission. I didn't have the concept of getting underneath and pushing up rather than pushing against and tearing apart. Submission is not about Curt controlling me or me giving up my independence. Rather, it is about love and sacrifice. It is about giving away the kind of love God has given me, and love is sacrifice. Ephesians 5:21 says, "Submit to one another out of reverence for Christ." This scripture goes on to describe how women and men should submit to one another. In Greek, submission means getting underneath and putting in order (Bell, p. 113). As Jack Frost puts it, it is to get underneath and push up. It is about sacrifice and surrender to everyone, and this includes the boss, the custodian, and the cashier. We submit out of reverence for Christ, not because they can do something for us. I know I have been guilty of doing something for someone in hopes that they would do something for me in return.

Hebrews 13:17 is a painful reminder of a time when I didn't understand submission. It reads:

> *Obey your leaders and submit to their authority. They keep watch over you as men who must give an account. Obey them so that their work will be a joy, not a burden, for that would be of no advantage to you.*

When I was younger, I worked for a summer ministry and once found myself in a difficult situation. I'd been hired for one ministry but had been assigned to a staff that had two ministry focuses for the summer. The person in charge of my team had no experience in one ministry area for which I'd been hired, home repair, though he did have experience in the other, day camp. In theory, we were to work together to accomplish our summer ministry assignments. I was offended by the change in my summer assignment and disgruntled to discover that my team leader had no experience with construction. I copped a major attitude, as I was quite young and foolish at the time, and instead of helping my team leader succeed, I made his life more difficult because I was angry. I essentially took over his responsibilities and wouldn't let him have any authority over our team. If someone would have shown me the scripture from Hebrews, I would have said, "Yeah, but..." My lack of submission affected everyone on our staff.

It is easy to look back on that summer and see how I could have handled the entire situation better. We could have worked together. I could have had a teachable attitude. I could have gotten underneath and pushed up rather than tearing the staff apart. I used to look at that summer as something of a personal attack, something that had been done to me, but I should have seen it as a difficult situation filled with opportunity. God has called us to submit to Him and to others. If I had submitted to my team leader, we would have built a relationship and had a far more successful summer. Instead, I was motivated by anger and resentment, so things did not go smoothly for either of us. If I had only known then what I know now!

Submission is now something I look at with joy and expectancy. It builds up people and the kingdom. It honors people and relationships first and makes way for humility and joy. Life has been a lot more fun since I've managed to take the focus off me and learned to look for ways to get underneath others and push up. Thank you, God, for another painful but life-giving lesson.

Identity

God had yet another lesson for me to learn. Part of living for God's kingdom and being dependent on my relationship with Him has meant dealing with where I find my identity. Apparently my identity wasn't where it should be. He showed me where I was finding my identity, and it was a hard pill to swallow. My identity was not in living for His kingdom, nor was it dependent on my relationship with Him.

Early one August Saturday, my husband called to inform me that his elderly grandfather, Papa, was going to move in with us. We've always had the understanding that our door would be open for such a situation so while I was shocked, I was also completely supportive of his decision. It was a whirl-wind to rearrange the house to accommodate Papa's needs, but he was out of the nursing home and with us by that Tuesday.

Curt was in charge of Papa's care. He arranged doctor appointments, set out his medication, and even took care of bathing him. In addition, we set up home healthcare to help us take care of his needs as there was a lot to keep track of and arrange. Before we knew it, September had arrived, and Curt had to go back to work.

We had talked about hiring someone to stay with Papa during the day, but we weren't ready for that step. I decided to take a leave of absence from my position at the church until we were more organized and had a better understanding of Papa's long-term needs. I spoke with the pastor as soon as possible, and he granted the leave without hesitation. As I left the church that afternoon, I looked at the secretary and said with tears in my eyes, "I am not a home healthcare provider." I was very nervous about caring for him as it was way out of my comfort zone.

In spite of my initial uneasiness about the situation, I loved having Papa at our house, and I was soon taking joy in providing some of the care Papa needed. Bringing him meals, checking his blood pressure, and giving him his meds were no problem. However, I was not prepared to bandage bedsores, clean up accidents, or help him change his clothes. Fortunately Curt was able to do most of this before and after school.

One day, though, the nurse had to show me a change in how his bandages were to be applied. Terrified, I went in to Papa's room. I watched and decided it wasn't so bad, that I could change his bandages if necessary, but bandages weren't the only change that needed to be made.

During my leave of absence from the church work, it became clear that God wanted me to stay home and care for Papa rather than hire someone else. I was freaking out on the inside as I'd been working in ministry for almost twenty years, and I'd been at my current church for eight years. It was all I had known professionally. *Who am I without ministry?* I wondered. I loved being in ministry, and the thought of giving it up left me feeling lost and empty, as if I were losing part of my very identity.

I gave God every reason I could think of to convince Him to let me keep my job at the church, but he patiently and gently knocked down every wall I threw up. I was left with a painful reality: For all of my adult life, I'd found my identity and purpose in ministry and not God. I felt as if God were stripping me of almost every last bit of independence I had. I know there is still some residue left that will surface at some point, but He will clean that too. Once I realized what God was doing, I asked Him to forgive my independence and to forgive me for looking to something other than Him for my identity. Then I resigned from my position at the church.

It was so hard to let go at the church, but staying home with Papa turned out to be one of the best things I have ever done. Trusting God over my fears brought me and my family great joy and many blessings. I wish it had lasted longer, as Papa passed away after a short six months with us. Now, I will always have my new identity and look to God for my new purpose; I must remember this so I don't go back to finding my identity in purpose. It is a habit I'll have to work on with Him.

Conclusion

Dusting the furniture, for me, has been about stripping myself of filth and residue in areas of my life that I hadn't even realized were dirty. I had become so used to how I felt that it seemed normal, and I had no idea I was capable of feeling so whole. Allowing God to refine me in these areas has been life-giving. Dusting has given me as much, if not more, than any other area of cleaning He has carried me through. My house wouldn't be clean without the finishing sparkle and shine.

Chapter 8

Vacuuming:
Get rid of religious junk

Vacuuming is one of those household chores that always needs to be done. I swear, I could do it daily at my house. I suppose I could get different carpet that doesn't show the dirt so easily, but I've learned it's best to clean the dirt rather than hide it.

Vacuuming involves suctioning dirt and grime out of the carpet and furniture, the debris left over from people walking on or sitting on it. It happens continuously since everyone who comes into the house leaves something behind, usually without even realizing it. Dirt sticks to our shoes and hands and is left behind everywhere we sit or walk. We can't help but leave a trail everywhere we go, and some people leave more dirt behind than others. Vacuuming is a way of cleaning it out and removing it.

If you haven't guessed it by now, the dirt I'm talking about refers to negative attitudes—the enemy getting in the way and pulling everyone down. Pessimists are easy to spot, and as soon as they walk into the room or office, hearts sink a little. Why? Because we know they'll have nothing positive to say about anything. As such, we're brought down a notch as soon as we see them. I admit that, at times, I am that Debbie Downer, but it is far less frequent than it used to be. I am better at catching myself before I pollute too many people, and I've also gotten better at apologizing when I go overboard.

What follows are some of the practices I've learned that have helped me further experience God's love, break ties to the wounding of the past, stay connected with God throughout my day, and live each moment with Him in mind. This required that I put aside the religious junk I'd been carrying around and look directly to Him and His Word for direction. Again, I am not perfect, but like any good habit, it takes practice and discipline. When I allow Christ to suck the filth off of me and vacuum me clean, I feel my energy restored, and that sticky, hazy film of negativity lifts. I think vacuuming is becoming my favorite chore.

Negativity

We have all walked into a room and felt the weight of negativity in the air, that cliché tension so thick it can be cut with a knife. We have also come to the end of a long day of work and felt like the life has been sucked out of us due, in part, to being surrounded by so much negativity.

I have spent most of my life ignoring the fact that we are all forms of energy. School taught us that the atom is the core of everything, but quantum physicists will now tell you that atoms can be split. When they start talking about subatomic particles (what is inside the atom) such as leptons, your brain may start to twitch like mine and threaten to explode. It sounds like science fiction, but researchers really have discovered a subatomic particle that can disappear, then reappear in a different spot without having to actually travel the distance in between (*Everything Is Spiritual*, Rob Bell).

And let's not forget about the effects of stress on the body. If the body cannot differentiate between emotional and physical stress, which it can't, and physical illness can result from emotional stress, isn't energy the core? (Colbert, p. 4) Bumper-to-bumper traffic, challenges at work, and our children's bad choices can all cause us stress, as they are all negative forces (energy) on the body, mind, and spirit. If we did more to control our response to stressors (because we can't control the stressors), wouldn't it result in greater health and wellbeing? It makes sense to me.

Why does the concept of energy working for health purposes seem so far fetched, so New Age? Is it really? What are we doing when we lay hands on someone, when we call on the Holy Spirit to fill or heal someone? It sounds like energy work to me, God's holy energy, energy created by the Creator of everything. This was where I had to start putting aside my religious junk and see that science does, in many ways, confirm exactly what scripture says.

The early church had healers in their ministries, but now we're on the other end of the spectrum, denying those forms of healing. God gave them to us, but we've allowed fear and misunderstanding (used so well by the enemy) to get in the way of our continued use of them. Be warned, and let me be clear: If you seek treatment from a healer, make sure he or she is grounded in Christ. Being grounded in Christ will allow the Holy Spirit to come in and do the work God wants done. Without that grounding, the door will be left open for the enemy, and we certainly don't need to give him any more opportunities to mess with our lives.

There is so much we can do every day to keep our energy level up and prevent others from leaving their dirt and grime on us. This chapter will cover several of them, but some of the "Doing Dishes" ideas also help. For example, I was once told by a Christian healer that I was giving my energy away, that I was letting other people take energy away from me and pull me down. Needless to say, I was a little skeptical at first, thanks to my religious junk, but she suggested the following: "Imagine a large cross about six feet in front of you. Next, imagine God's holy light going from the cross and over you, infinitely behind you." *Well,* I thought, *that can't hurt,* and I tried it. I would start my day that way, and when I felt my energy level dipping, I'd do it again, and the Holy Spirit would fill me up. It has been a great tool to refocus and reenergize myself. I was able to come home after a day of substitute teaching and still have energy for my family, something I had lost. It was also a moment to pause and refocus on kingdom purposes.

We also need to remember that the enemy loves to steal, rob, and destroy our joy, along with God's blessings. The enemy wants to suck us into the negative, dark situations around us. "What can we do about that?" you might ask. I've used the following methods to center my heart on God and His love. Some of them are simple, everyday ways to rid negativity, like the suggestion above. Some provide further cleansing in areas of our heart that God reveals to us.

Purification

Purification is a process of cleaning and making new. In this case, we are cleaning our hearts to make them new and full of God's love. Purification can happen in lots of different ways, and I have outlined a few I've worked with over the years. One may speak to you more than others, and one or two may be specifically helpful in the area you're cleaning. Trust the nudging of the Holy Spirit and go with what is on your heart; one process does not increase the work of the Holy Spirit over another. God is going to do what God is going to do. I don't think Jesus needed to spit in the blind man's eyes (Mark 8:23), and He didn't do that every time He healed blindness. All it did was symbolize that healing was taking place.

Visualization, as we discussed earlier, is a good example of how we can open ourselves up to God's love and healing. These processes of purification can help us open our heart to the work of the Holy Spirit. We have to be willing to let God into our heart because He's not going to ram his way in. Purification is about helping us receive what God already wants to give.

We are all aware of water and baptism. Water is another example of symbolic purification. When we are dirty, we want to be cleaned. To get clean, we wash ourselves. It can be really simple. Sometimes, especially when I've been going through a lot of emotional upheaval, it feels good to literally wash clean. Or if God shows me something I need to correct or repent for, I will literally jump in the shower and wash myself clean of it and pray through it while washing. When I am done, I feel clean and refreshed, both physically and spiritually.

Water can also be a dramatic way to symbolically represent the cleaning God is doing in our lives. Here is an example: Fill the bathtub and add olive oil or another essential oil if you'd like. Ask your spouse to wash you and pray over you for God's love and healing. Pray scriptures that are significant to your experience. If you don't have a spouse, do it yourself, knowing that God is the One who is cleansing you. This can be a powerful experience in moving forward.

Whether we have had a really bad day and need to wash ourselves clean of the negativity to start fresh or we need a dramatic cleansing with water by the Holy Spirit, it is another way for us to rid ourselves of the worldly junk and wrap ourselves in His holy embrace.

There are also forms of purification that scripture shows us as rituals before God. Anointing with oil and praying the blood of Jesus are forms of this. James 5:14-15 reminds us,

> *Is any one of you sick? He should call the elders of the church to pray over him and anoint him with oil in the name of the Lord. And the prayer offered in faith will make the sick person well; the Lord will raise him up. If he has sinned, he will be forgiven.*

Anointing with oil is used for more than healing sickness. In 2 Corinthians, believers are anointed. Many believe it is the physical manifestation of being continually filled with the Holy Spirit. Oil is also used with prayers for peace and protection, as well as to dedicate someone for ministry.

We don't have to be a ministry professional to anoint with oil. Using oil is another way for us to open ourselves up to receive what God has for us. Think of the beauty of anointing a young adult before they head off to college and praying into them all the promises God has for them. It will create a special memory to hold on to when life is hard, and it will make it all the easier for them to remember and hold on to God's promises.

We have started a new tradition in our family. At all bridal showers, we surround the bride and lay hands on her and pray over her all the blessings of marriage. It has become a bonding moment for the women of our family and a way of supporting the new bride. Anointing can take many forms and doesn't have to be limited to formal ministry.

Praying the blood of Jesus over someone or yourself is another form of purification. Jesus shed His blood for our freedom from sin and the enemy (John 8:36). Since then, people have been praying the blood of Jesus over people as a way of cleansing or sanctifying those being prayed for. Many scriptures identify the work of His blood: redeems and cleanses from sin (John 1:7, Ephesians 1:7); justifies (Romans 5:9, Hebrews 13:12); cleanses the mind (Hebrews 9:4); reconciles us with God (Romans 5:1); and enables us to approach God (Hebrews 10:19).

I understood the work of His blood cognitively. I understood why people prayed that over others, but once again, until it happened to me personally, it wasn't able to move into my heart.

I had been struggling with my body's need to hold on to yeast. This doesn't happen from eating too much bread, as one might think. Too much yeast in your system causes autoimmune diseases. I'd already had my gallbladder removed, due to scar tissue buildup, and my body was literally attacking itself. I didn't want to sit back and see what would be attacked next, but my body was holding on to the yeast for reasons unknown to me. So I prayed and asked God how to break the cycle within my body.

I focused on the Holy Spirit and was led to go through a generational repentance. I was led all the way back to

Exodus. God showed me that my family sat on their hands and refused to put the blood on the door as He instructed during the Passover. He also showed me that they ate bread with yeast when they were instructed not to. I repented for my generational line not following God's instructions, for their choice to go directly against God's will. He told me to pray the blood of Jesus over my children and myself, so I visualized His blood being poured out over our heads, and I praised God for cleansing us. I literally felt a cleansing wash over my body, and I knew instantly that the Holy Spirit was changing me physically. I felt light and free, and no longer need to take Candida, a supplement for yeast. Visualizing Jesus' blood pouring out opened my heart to receive what God wanted to pour out. It moved the experience out of my head and into my heart. I have finally learned that when my heart changes, I change. If I only have knowledge in my head, there is no change.

Authority

It is easy to forget that we have authority over the enemy. Dutch Sheets teaches in *Authority in Prayer*,

> The more we learn to function in the invisible spiritual realm, recognizing and applying its governing principles, the more we can partner with God, positively impact our world, avoid the snares and influence of the evil one, and enjoy the blessings of our salvation.

Mr. Sheets also teaches is that we have authority over the physical space we currently occupy. For example, when I am substitute teaching, I pray over the classroom when I enter it.

I invite the Holy Spirit to come in and tell the enemy to stay away. I declare my authority through Jesus Christ and proclaim that only that which is of God's holiness is welcome while I'm teaching. When I first did this, I noticed a marked difference in the atmosphere of the room. It reduced difficulties with students and brought a positive attitude to the space.

We have authority within our minds as well. In a book by Frances Frangiapane, *Three Battlefields,* the author addresses the negative thinking patterns in our minds. I have found his suggestion for the negative tapes I play in my mind very helpful. Mr. Frangiapane suggest that when we start saying to ourselves, "I can't do this," we are affirming what the enemy is telling us, agreeing with him and letting him know he is right. At this point we must declare that we stand in the light of the One who can do it. We must claim Jesus Christ, who died for us. He also suggests imagining standing in His light. This is another way of taking authority within our own mind; on many occasions, this has enabled me to stop my negative thinking patterns and has prevented me from becoming negative toward those around me.

Gratitude

Taking on an attitude of gratitude is a great way to see the positive, even in difficult situations. It also helps keep our energy up. We need to be thankful for all the gifts that are given to us and those around us each day. It is easy to be grateful for family and friends, and we can even be grateful for our jobs, but some gifts may not be so obvious. Are you grateful for taxes? I am, for without our tax dollars, we wouldn't have the protection of our fine military. We wouldn't have schools, protected national parks, Social Security, streets to drive on, and the list goes on. These systems are not perfect, and there is often much political unrest surrounding how they should be handled, but I am grateful to be able to do my part in supporting them. In all things, we must give thanks!

An attitude of gratitude is also a gift to those around us. I would rather leave gratitude behind than the grime of complaining. How the world would change if each of us managed to get 50 percent better at being thankful and showing gratitude to others. Thank the custodian who cleans for you, tell a co-worker you appreciate their hard work, or thank a server at a restaurant, and we can change the world.

Conclusion

Deciding to take control of the energy we send out to others can dramatically change how we experience each day. When I choose not to receive other people's bad day, I can stay positive. When the world throws up on me, lets me have it, or calls me names, I don't have to let it ruin my entire day. When I find myself heading down the path of being negative and crabby, I seek the source of the negativity and ask God to show me how to change it. Sometimes I need to be thankful, and other times, I need to repent and start over, or at least reassess where my negative attitude is coming from. Nowadays, I have more control over my daily experiences than I ever thought possible. I don't have to let things happen to me. It has taken a willingness to let go of the religious junk I thought I understood and look closely at scripture and Him.

Chapter 9

Doing Dishes: Brimming with worship

Do you like to do dishes? I have to say it's my least favorite household chore. I'd rather mop floors. Maybe it is because dishes pile up every day, since most families are always eating. My kitchen always needs to be cleaned up. "Can't they take a day off?" I often ask, but if I take a day off from the dishes, there's quite a mess left for me the next day. I'm one of those people whose insides are a little agitated if there are dishes everywhere. I feel so much better when everything is cleaned up and I can finally feel at rest.

Doing dishes is all about the things we need to do daily in life to enjoy spiritual health and rest. We are told to worship Him in everything we do. When I am spiritually healthy, I'm brimming with worship. I am better at giving love away. I am nicer to be around, and my day stays focused on God.

Doing dishes, however, is not meant to be prescriptive or ritualistic. I really believe God wants a natural relationship with us; only then can our worship truly flow naturally and meaningfully, not forced. He doesn't want us to come to Him out of obligation but out of desire. There are days when the dishes just don't get done; my routine in spending time with God may change, and that's okay. It is not about the amount of time spent seeking God and studying the Word. It's about my heart. Just like when I am agitated because there are dishes everywhere, I also get agitated when I do not spend time with God daily. As I consider this, I have to believe that perhaps He's hardwired us in such a way that the more we worship and stay connected to Him, the easier it is to face what life throws at us.

In addition to spending time with God, there are a couple other things that will really enhance our daily lives: laughter and hugs. These are life-giving, never draining, and are amazing for our overall health. They build on the vacuuming we did in the last chapter. We can't just get rid of negativity; instead, we have to replace it with something. Hugs, laughter, joy, and hearing the voice of God are wonderful replacements. Just thinking about it makes my day better. So grab the soap, washcloth, and a towel. It's time to soak our hands in some living water and then spread it around to all those we meet throughout the day. If we're not careful, doing dishes might actually start to sound like fun!

Things I Do Daily

I have discovered that there are things we need to do daily in our lives as we walk as children of God, things that will allow us to live as closely as possible to "on earth as it is in heaven." Okay, it won't be exactly like that, but there are certainly moments when I feel like I've found a little piece of heaven, and I do believe there is a place for hugs, laughter, and joy in our daily lives, along with hearing the voice of God. The attitude we take on each day can be one driven by Him or one driven by the world. The days I choose to let him drive are so much better!

Hugs

We must hug each other, as shaking hands is not enough. We need a holy embrace. Our society has become so violated by litigation that we are afraid to touch each other, let alone give someone a hug. Still, we need touch. Hugs are not just for little children. We all need hugs to live. I won't suggest that caution doesn't need to be exercised in certain situations, as I spent many years being uncomfortable with hugs due to being violated. Even now, I often hold back out of fear of being socially inappropriate, but I can do better at taking advantage of situations where it is appropriate.

There is a lot of research on the need for touch, particularly regarding infants and children. Carmen Jochmann states, in an article for *Healthfield*, that touch is vital to the positive health and development of all humans, regardless of age. Humans have a need for touch, almost as strong as our need for food and water (2009). Studies have even been conducted on the elderly and touch. Therapist and author Virginia Satir is often quoted as saying human beings need four hugs a day for survival, eight for maintenance, and twelve for growth (http://www.brainyquote.com/quotes/keywords/hugs.html). If I didn't have kids at home, I'd never reach twelve!

Hugs, though, are more than touch. An embrace represents compassion, caring, and love. Hugs are important because they are a way to express love to one another, a way for us to show someone we care and that we're glad to see them. So let's get out there and greet one another with a holy embrace.

Laughter

Doesn't it feel good to laugh? It energizes us and lightens burdens. As a little girl, I often saw my dad reading *Reader's Digest*. I enjoyed folding the magazines into Christmas trees, but I also liked to read the "Laughter Is the Best Medicine" section and chuckle. I always feel so alive after a good laugh, and Proverbs 17:22 assures us, "A merry heart is good medicine."

I really learned the value of laughter in my early college days. I was working with a ministry called Mountain TOP, a youth mission project in the Tennessee Mountains, serving with their summer staff. Each week a hundred or more teens and adults showed up at camp to serve through building projects or to provide a day camp experience for the local children. I've mentioned this story before, but it begs repeating that I was highly uncomfortable in the day camp ministry. I was so out of my comfort zone that I cried every day of the first week of day camp, but since I didn't want the campers to notice my discomfort, I managed to plaster on a fake smile around them.

In the second week of day camp, I was prepared for another week of the same emotional experience. A group had brought a huge box of books for the week, and while I was digging through it, I found a Calvin and Hobbes book by Bill Watterson. I had never read the comic before, but it immediately brought a real smile to my face, and I carried that book with me the rest of the summer. During that week of day camp, I took time everyday to laugh with Calvin, and that eliminated my tears. God didn't take away my discomfort, but through that book of comics, He gave me a tool to handle it, and that was a huge gift.

Even the medical community supports that laughter has many benefits for our overall health. Dr. Lee Berk, of Loma Linda University Medical Center, has studied laughter and concludes that it reduces stress hormones, lowers blood pressure, and boosts the immune system (*Deadly Emotions*). He also showed that growth hormone, also known as the youth hormone, increased an astonishing 87 percent in those who laughed frequently. Forget wrinkle cream, I just need to laugh more. Dr. Colbert (*Deadly Emotions*) actually prescribes laughter to his patients and also notes that laughter is good exercise. It allows for deep-breathing as in aerobic exercise. Lastly, he states that it is good for the brain in that it allows both the right and left sides to work simultaneously.

Laughter is contagious and should be shared with others, and it can be a great testimony as to the joy the Lord gives. As Psalm 126:2-3 tells us,

> *Our mouths were filled with laughter, our tongues with songs of joy. Then it was said among the nations, "The Lord has done great things for them." The Lord has done great things for us, and we are filled with joy.*

Perhaps laughter's contagious nature is why we must share a good joke with others when it makes us burst into laughter.

It is also good to laugh at ourselves. Sometimes this can be difficult or embarrassing, but it can eliminate negative emotions and shame. While I was substitute teaching in biology, the students were tasked to identify the parts of a cell. I asked the class what the blue spheres were, except I used the word "balls" instead of spheres. In an instant, that room full of teenagers fell apart with laughter. Of course, I made the mistake of telling my husband, the math teacher, and the next day, he shared it with the math department. A lot of people had a good laugh at my verbal faux pas, but I had to be able to laugh along with them. Honestly, I had a hard time holding in my own laughter as the students were roaring with it.

How simple is it to laugh more? It is an easy, free thing to do that will reduce stress and anxiety. I think I need to take time to read more of the jokes that end up in my inbox because laughter really is the best medicine!

Hearing the Voice of God

There is nothing better than hearing the voice of God and knowing with confidence that it is Him you are hearing. Throughout my life, I've had a few very memorable experiences when God has spoken to me or through me. One of the most memorable was when He told me to write this book. I'd always wanted to hear Him more often, but I assumed He'd get around to talking to me when He had some glorious thing for me to do. I felt that way because I was still living in a Master/servant relationship rather than the Father/daughter relationship I have now. When He told me to write this book, His voice was very clear. I felt like I was talking to the sky. I was looking up, but I heard His voice in my head. Other times, I have heard a whisper in my ear, literally an audible voice. So many Christian friends have asked, "Wait…you actually hear God? I don't." I tell them, "You can, if you'll only listen."

I have since learned that God wants to speak to me every day, and I have learned how to posture myself to hear more clearly. Mark Virkler does a teaching series on hearing the voice of God every day, a very practical approach to listening and journaling. He teaches how to focus on Christ and hear God's voice, and it is a wonderful technique. It was awkward for me at first, and I had to modify it slightly, since I can't seem to journal and listen to God at the same time; I have to listen and then write.

Mr. Virkler also taught me to pay attention to spontaneous thoughts. If they are positive, I attribute them to God and act on them. If I have an aha moment, I attribute that to God speaking to me as well.

I have also started journaling my dreams. God still speaks to us in dreams and visions, and many scriptures tell of this. The following one, Acts 2:17, can also be found in the book of Joel:

"In the last days," God says, "I will pour out my Spirit on all people. Your sons and daughters will prophesy, your young men will see visions, your old men will dream dreams."

We should all find a decent, trustworthy Christian resource for dream interpretation. James Goll's *Dream Language* is one, as he provides biblical understanding of dream interpretation, along with tools to help begin interpreting dreams. It is fun to see what God is telling me while I sleep, though I've found it difficult, at times, to figure it out. When I do, I always discover profound encouragement and guidance.

God hasn't stopped speaking to us, but how are we to do His will if we can't hear Him guiding us? Isn't conversation part of a personal relationship? Nowhere in scripture does it say He has stopped talking to us. It's just that most of us haven't learned how to listen. Learning to listen can help us to be confident in the choices we make, knowing that they are what God wants for our life.

Choices and discernment can be a tricky, narrow road to walk. God doesn't want us to be robots, yet He wants to lead us. Quite frankly, I would prefer Him to steer me rather than me being in control of my own destiny. There are certainly a lot of adventures in my life that never would have happened had I been in control. He recently had to remind me that He wants to steer, so I put a reminder on my cell phone screen to remind me daily to ask Him to. I can't say that He has always been in the front, but life is much better when He is. In Tim Hansel's book, *Holy Sweat*, there is a great poem that I have been trying to live by for over twenty years:

The Road of Life *(by unknown author)*

At first, I saw God as my observer, my judge,
keeping track of the things I did wrong,
so as to know whether I merited Heaven or Hell when I die.
He was out there sort of like a president.
I recognized His picture when I saw it,
But I really didn't know Him.

But later on
when I met Christ,
it seemed as though life were rather like a bike ride,
but it was a tandem bike,
and I noticed that Christ
was in back helping me pedal.

I don't know just when it was
that He suggested we change places,
but life has not been the same since.

When I had control,
I knew the way.
It was rather boring,
but predictable...
It was the shortest distance between two points.
       But when He took the lead,
He knew delightful long cuts,
up mountains,
and through rocky places
at breakneck speeds,
it was all I could do to hang on!
Even though it looked like madness,
He said, "Pedal!"
       I worried and was anxious
and asked, "Where are you taking me?"
He laughed and didn't answer,
And I learned to trust.
       I forgot my boring life
and entered into the adventure.
And when I'd say, "I'm scared,"
He'd lean back and touch my hand.
       He took me to people with gifts that I needed,
gifts of healing, acceptance, and joy.
They gave me gifts to take on my journey,
my Lord's and mine.
       And we were off again.
He said, "Give the gifts away;
they're extra baggage, too much weight."
So I did,
to the people we met,
and I found that in giving I received,
and still our burden was light.

I did not trust Him,
at first,
in control of my life.
I thought He'd wreck it;
but He knows bike secrets,
knows how to make it bend to take sharp corners,
knows how to jump to clear high rocks,
knows how to fly to shorten scary passages.
    And I am learning to shut up and pedal
in the strangest places,
and I'm beginning to enjoy the view
and the cool breeze on my face
with my delightful constant companion, Jesus Christ.
    And when I'm sure I just can't do anymore,
He just smiles and says…. "Pedal."

Sometimes I have to remind myself, "Shut up and pedal!" Mostly though, I simply ask Him to steer me daily. I seem to get more done and with a better attitude when I first say, "Steer me, Lord."

Choose Joy

Exactly what is joy? We seem to know it when we see it and feel it, but it's quite difficult to define. Joy is not the same as happiness. It is something that comes from deeper within us, something intimate that can even be felt when we're experiencing deep pain. "Joy is abiding and enduring," says Don Colbert (*Deadly Emotions* p. 186).

Even though the world tells us we should live in pursuit of happiness, happiness is dependent on our external circumstances. We need to do something or receive something to make us feel happy. Watching my husband clean up the kitchen makes me happy, but it doesn't give me joy. There is joy in our relationship, but that is due to our connectedness. When my sons clean their rooms, I am happy, but the joy in my heart for them comes from the depth of my love for them. Perhaps we should all be demanding life, liberty, and the pursuit of...joy!

> Joy is a choice, as Don Colbert says in *Deadly Emotions*: Joy does not flow from situations. It flows from your will and our emotions deep within. You can choose to be joyful, or you can choose to be miserable. Nobody can make these inner choices for you (p. 188).

Pain and difficult circumstances afford us the chance to choose joy. We can choose to live in bitterness and sadness, or we can celebrate God in all things. When we praise God in the darkest moments, we will truly tap into His joy. In the Greek, being blessed is the deepest quality of joy. The Bible says, "Blessed are those who mourn." Mourning is certainly a place of pain, yet He is willing to give us joy in place of that. We make the choice to praise and give thanks to God in all things, and in the midst of mourning, it may be very difficult to choose joy. Maybe that is why God chooses to bless us with the deepest quality of joy in those moments when we need it most. So how do we do it? Tim Hansel, who has dealt with severe daily pain since an accident, puts it this way in *Holy Sweat*:

> Choosing joy doesn't alleviate the pain, the ambiguity or the doubt. It just gives you a way to live with it.... Joy is that deep settled confidence that God is in con-

trol of every area of your life...Joy is free, but not cheap. It takes an intimate relationship with courage, with faith and more often than not with pain...I simply contend that joy is a better option, at the low points of your life as well as the high. And as you choose joy it becomes easier to choose it the next minute, the next hour, the next day, the next year. When you've got joy, you've got it all (pp. 137-138).

Does that make it easier? I say we fake it until we make it, and we may have to do that every minute of every hour. Remember, though, that we don't have to do it alone, for we can lean on the One who is the fullness of joy. Psalm 16:11 reminds us,

You will make known to me the path of life; in Your presence is fullness of joy; In Your right hand, there are pleasures forever (NASB).

Also, we are reminded in Nehemiah 8:10b that we will find our strength in His joy: "Do not be grieved, for the joy of the Lord is your strength." We don't choose joy alone. We choose joy through Him, the One who is our joy and our strength. But why choose joy? One obvious answer is that few people enjoy being around those who are miserable. I don't even want to be around myself when I am miserable. Choosing joy gives us strength and draws us into the fullness of God. In essence, it represents our choice to cast our misery on Him and take back His joy. I think that might be how we receive the peace that surpasses all understanding, by allowing God to work within us in the midst of pain and sorrow. It is true that sometimes we have to fake it until we make it; we have to choose it every minute till we can make it an hour, but we will get there. He will give us the joy.

Another reason to choose joy is for the benefit of others. Everything we have been given from God (grace, love, mercy) is meant to be given away, and joy is among these pass-along gifts. Choosing joy allows us to submit to others with joy. When we do that, we will share that joy with others. It is as great to give as it is to receive. Some people instantly make me smile because they have a great attitude that is genuine to who they are. They choose joy, and I benefit from it.

We live in a world that could use more joy. When I choose to change my attitude, I feel better on the inside, and I know that is being projected on the outside. When I choose joy, I choose to lean with confidence on the One who freely gives it.

Conclusion

Who knew doing dishes could be so life-giving? Growing up, I was taught to talk to God, do devotions, and read my Bible at least daily. Unfortunately, these always came across to me as chores on a to-do list somewhere. I'm not saying we shouldn't do those things. Doing dishes is not a chore for me when my heart is focused on worship. What is not to love about a big bear hug and belly laugh? They certainly don't feel like chores. Learning to hear God's voice has given me a new sense of closeness to Him. Now, I look forward to every moment I get to spend with Him, and I must say I feel a great wealth of natural joy these days. Of course, there are those days and moments when I must consciously choose joy, but doing dishes brings light and life to my day. A sparkling clean kitchen brings me more than peace. It brings me joy.

Chapter 10

Cobwebs in the Corner:
Not an indifferent bystander

Cobwebs are so easy to miss because they're light and thin and blend in so easily with their surroundings. Every once in a while, the light shines at just the right angle, and we see them as if they'd appeared out of nowhere. We wonder how they went unnoticed, since they suddenly seem so obvious, and we're immediately compelled to get a broom or a rag and get rid of them.

Cobwebs are funny that way, aren't they? The good thing is that they're quite easy to get rid of. One swipe with a rag, and they're gone. We might think we're done cleaning cobwebs, only to see another one pop up, but at least it isn't so daunting to deal with because they're so easy to clean. When the light shines on it, it's simple to bring God's cleansing to it.

Some cobwebs, though, take a little more work. Sometimes they pop up when we don't see them coming. If we walk through a cobweb we didn't see, it will stick to us, wrap around us, and get in our faces. It's nearly impossible to shake it off because the cobweb won't let go. These can take slightly more work to clean up, but we really want them gone, because we know what it's like to feel clean and cobweb-free. To get out of such a sticky mess, hopefully we're willing to take the extra time to dig in and deal with the issue God is showing us.

That is what living free is like. We see a cobweb in the corner and take care of it with one or two swipes. An issue pops up in life, and we can deal with it. Sometimes it might take a little more work than that, but now we have new tools to work through the mess, new eyes to see it through. Nothing looks the same anymore, and life is suddenly easier. Before, I spent months trying to clean up a cobweb or years in denial there was one across my face. Cobwebs will always show up from time to time, but that is part of the ongoing cleaning process God takes us through.

This chapter is about recognizing new areas God would like to clean and new ways of choosing to live after being wounded again. Remember, God is not an indifferent bystander. He will not waste an opportunity to bring us closer to Him through more cleaning. Even our burdens can be lifted if we let God bear them. God has given me some new ways of thinking to continue to refine me into the person He created me to be. Who would have thought swiping down cobwebs could actually be fun?

Living Free

Life isn't all about me. It is truly about God and His kingdom. I have a new way to pray, a new way to live. I see life with new eyes, and that continues to grow and develop within me as I study and seek the Holy Spirit to guide everything I do. The beauty is that this freedom is available to everyone who seeks it.

I have received many new tools to help me live each day in relationship with God and others. Don't be fooled, for I am in no way perfect. I have simply learned how to be a better listener to God, I find it easier to trust God, and I'm equipped with new tools to break old habits of behavior. There are definitely a few that still need breaking, as I'm sure my husband could tell you. God keeps revealing more areas for me to work on. I always knew it was going to be a lifelong process, but now I know He wants me to share the tools with others who are also on this ride.

I have learned that we can't force healing. God is in control, and it is about His timing. I have really come to believe that healing happens in layers so that we can take time to soak up every lesson that is revealed. There are also times when I have to revisit old lessons to learn them on a deeper level. Some of my roots are really deep. For me, worthiness and forgiving myself were those kinds of lessons I revisited several times before I felt a breakthrough in my heart. His willingness to repeat Himself time and time again continually reminds me how great God's love is for all of us.

Relationships are easier now because I don't worry about what others think of me. I no longer worry about people liking me, and I don't feel like I have to do everything right. I see others differently as well. I try to see people for who they are in God's eyes. Others are also wounded and in need of God's loving embrace, and their woundedness has softened me. I know now that hurt people hurt people, so when someone does something that hurts me, I try to see their pain rather than take their offense personally. Be prepared, my friend, for there will be more cobwebs and wounds to deal with on this road of life. I just keep trying to use my new cleaning products rather than go back to my old, rusty ones, and some days are easier than others.

As I've said, it's inevitable that I will be offended again, and I've also come to terms with the fact that I will never reach perfection in this life. Now, though, I have a choice when I am wounded. Do I hold a pity party for myself and head down a road that leads to a cycle of pain, or do I choose healing? I guarantee you I will do both. Hopefully, when I choose the road of pain, I won't be on that road long before I'll turn and choose healing and forgiveness.

It is also inevitable that I will wound someone else. I pray that when I do, I'll quickly realize my errors and choose restitution and repentance. The goal with these new tools is for me to continually strive to spend more and more of my days abiding in His love rather than in mistrust and fear. I want to continue to break old habits and become better and better at expressing His love to others.

I continue to work on catching orphan thinking, searching for habits and strongholds that need to change, and trying to suffer as Christ suffered. These new tools are really skills, and skills require continual practice and honing. Even as I strive to do better at them, I still slump and have low points. It is like playing an instrument. If I put it down for a while, my skill level backslides a little. I don't lose it all, and once I pick it up again and start practicing, I can return to the previous level rather quickly. Then the next thing I know I am making progress again. So if I forget to practice for a while, I just need to pick it up and get going. I know this happens to all of us.

Catch Orphan thinking

We've mentioned orphan thinking before, but what is it? I went through a ministry experience with Shiloh Place Ministries and, as I mentioned before, read the book *From Spiritual Slavery to Spiritual Sonship* by Jack Frost, founder of Shiloh Place. This process had a profound effect on how I view my relationship with Jesus and Father God. I had always seen God as my Master and myself as His servant. These teachings showed me that Jesus not only came for salvation but also to show us how to be in relationship with the Father as sons and daughters. I am striving to live each day as the daughter He loves and cherishes, for He said, "I have loved you with an everlasting love; I have drawn you with loving kindness" (Jeremiah 31:3b).

As His children, we have the right to His comfort and peace continually, to hear Him speak to us and guide our words and actions. He wants us to live in the embrace of His perfect love. He wants us to be at home in His love.

Home is where you can go and hear the voice of your Father say, "No matter what anybody else says, you are the child I love and on whom My favors rests." Home is where you constantly hear the voice of God speak His affirmation over you, His love over you, and His forgiveness, compassion, and grace over you. (*From Spiritual Slavery to Spiritual Sonship* p. 25).

Letting God fully into our hearts is the hard part. If your heart is not at home in love, Frost would call that orphan thinking.

Living like an orphan means struggling constantly with the fear of trusting. It is a life of independence, one in which we believe we are completely on our own. It means living in a state of agitated resistance against people who do not think like us. If we believe God is mad at us and that we must always find ways to appease Him, we will live like orphans. This is an important distinction, because however we think God feels about us is how we will treat others in our everyday relationships (p. 26).

I can't say I am constantly at home in love. It is part of the process, an area in which I continually strive to do better. I still catch myself drifting into orphan thinking, and sometimes I am knee deep in it. The good news is that we can always return home. Writing this book really opened my eyes to how God feels about me.

One of the biggest issues I have with staying at home in love is trust. Isn't trust hard sometimes? It is easy for me to say I trust God, but so often I try to take back control and do not trust God to handle it. *Life's Healing Choices* (Baker 2007) states that we can't trust God until we completely understand Him. I don't know if I will ever completely understand Him, but it makes sense to me. *The Shack* is another great book, an example of the true nature of God, even in life's darkest moments. It blows the door open on how big God's love really is for us. Having this bigger understanding of God's love makes it easier for me to trust Him with the areas of my life I still want to control, as if I could do a better job than Him. Tearing down the walls that prevent me from trusting Him has been a continual process of opening my heart to love. One thing is for sure: The more I've placed my complete trust in him, the more my heart has been able to feel His love for me.

Habits

We all have habits, both good and bad. Exercise is one of my good habits, and chocolate is one of my bad ones. A habit is a usual state, either acquired or is natural, and both good and bad habits require a mindset. In other words, whether conscious or subconscious, the mind has been set to see and act in a certain way. Have you ever set your mind on something? That is what I did with exercise. I decided to make a lifestyle change and build a new habit. Exercise would become part of my life, a minimum of four times a week. It was easy at first, and I was really motivated, but by the fourth week, I was reminding myself why I had chosen to make that change in my life. My motivation had dwindled, and I had to talk myself into going through my workout. Since then, more than seven years have gone by, and some weeks, it is still hard. It is a conscious decision every time.

Conscious decisions only make up 10 percent of our actions and attitudes; that leaves 90 percent that happen spontaneously. Second Corinthians 10:4-5 reminds us that we need to continually take every thought captive as we grow in obedience to Christ:

> *The weapons we fight with are not the weapons of the world. On the contrary, they have divine power to demolish strongholds. We demolish arguments and every pretension that sets itself up against the knowledge of God, and we take captive every thought to make it obedient to Christ.*

This can feel like a lot of work, and we have to remember that habits have voices that talk to us. I recently gave up Diet Coke, particularly because of aspartame. Diet Coke was my favorite, and after I gave it up, I'd see a can in the fridge staring at me, begging me to drink it: "Here I am. Don't you want to drink me?" I'd stare back at it for a moment then close the fridge. Thankfully, I physically felt better not drinking it, and that helped me close the fridge. It's hard to turn off those voices though.

Sometimes it helps to take a personal inventory of our behavior. I look at the fruits of my behavior and decide if I need to go after the root (Matthew 15:13). A friend of mine often says, "If you've got the fruit, you've got the root." I have to ask myself if the fruit is good or bad. I ask, "Is God showing me an area where roots need to be dug up? Are there thoughts I need to hold captive? Is there a habit that needs to change?"

Many habits/mindsets are unconscious. They have been a part of our lives for so long that there is no longer a conscious decision made when the situation arises. These can be the hardest habits to break. Our character is basically is a composite of our habits. As the maxim goes: Sow a thought, reap an action; sow an action, reap a habit; sow a habit, reap a character; sow a character, reap a destiny (*Seven Habits of Highly Effective People*, Steven Covey). So we need to continually renew our minds to change our habits. Romans 12: 2 warns,

> *Do not conform any longer to the pattern of this world, but be transformed by the renewing of your mind. Then you will be able to test and approve what God's will is— his good, pleasing and perfect will.*

Sometimes there are underlying strongholds, as mentioned in 2 Corinthians that need to be addressed before we can change a habit. Strongholds are habitual lies that we have embraced at the core of our inner being, built on a foundation of half-truths. They have become a fortress of thoughts that influence the way we respond to the truth about God's character within us, and they are not all demonic in nature (*Breaking Free* by Jack Frost). Our unconscious thoughts make up 90 percent of our actions and attitudes. We need to renew the spirit of our minds to be able to see the strongholds that are holding us back. In *The Amplified Bible*, we read in Ephesians 4:22-24:

> *Strip yourselves of your former nature [put off and discard your old un-renewed self] which characterized your previous manner of life and becomes corrupt through lusts and desires that spring from delusion; and be constantly renewed in the spirit of your mind [having a fresh mental and spiritual attitude], and put on the new nature (the regenerate self) created in God's image, [Godlike] in true righteousness and holiness.*

In *Breaking Free,* Shiloh Place Ministries identifies eight common ways strongholds are built:

- Passed down from generation to generation
- Built from deep hurts resulting from wounds
- By a misinterpretation of love, how we perceive love or rejection
- By judgments or inner vows we make toward ourselves, others, or God
- Through the words people speak over us
- Through false doctrine or false teaching
- Through our ethnic and cultural backgrounds
- By negative thinking patterns and false belief structures

This means a personal inventory might be a very daunting task. I have learned to let God guide my healing and refining, and He's doing a really great job! Apparently, I have a lot to refine. When God's in charge, we can handle what He has for us. Success in changing these habits/mindsets only happens when we get to the root, or we will continue to produce the fruit. I ask God to reveal the root so I can break the stronghold/habit.

We talked about the victim spirit earlier, but some of us also have a victim mindset. We may have negative thinking patterns or false beliefs about ourselves that we need to change. Maybe there are patterns in our relationships that are destructive rather than life-giving. I once had the mindset that I was trapped and couldn't do anything about my circumstances. Making changes in these areas, with God's help, can make profound differences in our relationships.

Changing our habits and being refined into the likeness of Christ is part of our continued journey with God. We need to continually renew the spirit of our minds.

Still, there is more. Does this sound familiar?

I do not understand what I do. For what I want to do, I do not do, but what I hate I do (Rom. 7:15 TNIV).

I know that feeling, and so did Paul. These are related to negative strongholds that we attribute to the list above and are more complicated than refusing to drink Diet Coke anymore. I'd be very wealthy if I had a nickel for every time I've said to myself, "That's just the way I am...I'm just a worrier...I don't deserve it...I'm not worth that kind of love." We all harbor underlying, unconscious statements that we live out, and we do it thinking that it's simply who we are. I've discovered I don't have to live like that anymore. Those were lies I bought into and repeated to myself, often in subtle ways. This doesn't mean I don't ever worry, but my worry is more appropriate to the situation, and I give it over to God more quickly.

For a long time, I struggled with understanding strong-holds. Some people use the term "ungodly soul ties." God, in His infinite wisdom, helped me see this at work in my own life. A couple of years had gone by since I'd experienced any rage or out-of-control anger. However, I was frustrated with my son's behavior when a flash went through my brain of me spanking him. I asked God what was going on. He had taken the rage from me, yet something had brought back that vision. I wondered if He was trying to teach me something and thought I might be missing the lesson. I had closed the generational attachment, so there was only one other thing it could be: a stronghold.

I had watched the Rob Bell video, *Everything Is Spiritual* and he'd introduced me to an area of quantum physics called string theory. Let me try to make it simple. The theory is based in mathematics. Let's start with how small the strings are: The universe is to earth as earth is to an atom as an atom is to a string. They are really small, one-dimensional particles that vibrate as they move (Wikipedia). They have energy and attach one to another and make a string. Strings are everywhere, going to and from everything, even from person to person. When I get angry at my son, I send out strings that attach to him, and this creates a stronghold to anger. It is important to note that there can be good strongholds that come from the positive things we do, but this anger was not one of them.

String theory helped us to develop our understanding of dimensions. It is easy for us to understand two and three dimensions, as we live in a three-dimensional world, but at least eleven dimensions have been discovered thus far. That is more than my brain can handle, but it helped me see that there is a connectedness between all of us. There are energies around us (angels, the Holy Spirit) that operate in other dimensions. The concept of strings helped me see how strongholds develop and how breaking them can bring increased freedom in Christ.

It is like picking up on someone's bad habit. My son acts out, and I get angry. He responds back in anger because that is what he has learned from me, and then, all of the sudden, we find ourselves in a cycle that has become a habit.

We always joke with my sister that she is just like our mom. It would be fair to say my mom is a little anxious and frets over almost everything—a trait my sister definitely picked up from her. This could be seen as a learned behavior, but I'm beginning to see this is only part of the answer. Habits have a life of their own. My sister responds to situations with anxiety before she has a chance to think about it; clearly, there is more at work here.

Let's go back to my anger example. For about a week prior, I'd been very short and snippy with my kids. I seem to have these spells often. I realized I shouldn't be reacting to them so negatively all the time, and I was reacting without thinking about it; words came out of my mouth before I even took time to filter them. It was a bad habit I'd been working on but with limited success. Once God started to teach me about strongholds, I realized I had a stronghold to anger and rage, and I found new success. I broke the stronghold to anger and rage in the name of Jesus, threw it under the feet of Jesus, then asked the Holy Spirit to restore me to the person I was created to be.

I think God used to the vision to get my attention and teach me about strongholds because once I broke them, I had a filter. I was finally able to adjust the tone of my voice before it came out of my mouth. It had always been easy for me to get snippy, and I knew it was a habit I needed to take more seriously when my oldest son asked me if he'd done something wrong because I sounded angry toward him. It had become my natural response. Now that those strongholds have been broken, I am far more successful at controlling my tone of voice, and the urge to snip has greatly reduced. It has made breaking this habit easier. Again, I am still not perfect, but I am improving.

I have also found some keys to success with strongholds. Asking for forgiveness and repentance are keys to preventing new negative strongholds from being built. When we ask someone to forgive us, it breaks the negativity between us and brings restoration to the relationship. It makes sense, then, that it breaks and restores any negative strongholds previously established.

Sometimes strongholds show up as walls around us. I have talked about walls before, and we know our own natural defenses cause us to build them around ourselves for protection. When a person in our life continually hurts us, we put up an emotional wall to keep them at a distance so their actions won't have an effect on us. The problem is that the wall keeps others at a distance as well, including God. It stands to reason that if the wall keeps God's love at a distance, the wall is spiritual, comprised of energy. Not only can we break the walls by opening our heart and rebuilding relationships, but we can further break them down by visualizing the wall around us. Once we see it God will help us notice just how high or thick it is. Through the power of Christ, we can start kicking and punching it down. I always ask the Holy Spirit to heal and restore me after any type of healing to lock the good work in my heart. This probably seems a little crazy, but when my walls of Jericho tumbled, I felt a great sense of relief inside.

Breaking strongholds in all areas of our lives can help us break the bad habits. Our negative habits don't have to have a chokehold on us anymore. We might think this is a small thing, and that there's no point in bothering. After all, habits are hard to break, and it takes diligence and commitment to break them. Why not make it easier? Why not get rid of all the residuals of anger or anxiety? Why not restore all areas God shows us? He's not indifferent to our lives. Everything we go through matters to Him. The more I've done this and opened my heart to Him, the more love I've had to give to others, especially my family.

Conclusion

Cobwebs need to be dealt with, or else they will get bigger and more prominent in our lives. It is tempting to say we'll deal with it later, but that won't make it go away. When God makes us aware of a habit such as our orphan thinking, it is so we will refine ourselves to be more like Him.

Every big or little cobweb I've gotten rid of has lightened my heart and brought me closer to God. The process sets me free and gives me an even greater understanding of how big God's (Daddy's) love is for all of us. I won't ignore cobwebs anymore because I love the freedom I have without them.

Chapter 11

Cleaning House: A Lifestyle

In case you haven't noticed, cleaning house is a lifelong process. God always wants us to learn about new areas within ourselves, our relationship with Him, and our relationships with others. Often, trying to understand God and our relationship with Him can be complex. As you continue to clean your house, here are some aha moments I've had, which I offer to you as final thoughts.

Suffering

I was out on a long walk near my house when I felt this strange urge to run. Something within me said, "Run! Do it!" First, I have to say that my body is not built for speed. Also, I've already had two knee surgeries. My first thought was that running would hurt; I was certain my knees would start to scream with pain. Then I heard, "They won't. I'm right here with you. Trust me." Ugh! I could sense Jesus' presence, and He was pushing me to run. He told me to stay on the dirt shoulder of the road and assured me I'd make it back to the driveway without pain. I was starting to question my sanity in practicing Mark Virkler's method for hearing the voice of God, but I obeyed what I heard. In the end, my legs were burning, but there was no pain in my knees.

I wondered what that running was all about. I was definitely frustrated with my weight again. I'd been diagnosed with low thyroid, just like all of my siblings, and I knew something was wrong when I gained seven pounds in one week. I was working hard to get the weight off, and I was willing to run if that was what it would take. So I started walking/running twice a week as part of my regular workouts. It was great God time, but the funny thing was, I think God had something more in mind.

We were up in northern Minnesota at Curt's grandpa's cabin, and I decided to go for a walk/run. I knew there was a dirt road I could run on, since I could run without pain if I stayed off the pavement, and I'd walk the rest of the way. I ran down the road and back and decided to continue walking down the main road. Off in the distance, I saw a dirt road with a big, long hill, and I heard, "You can do it!" I thought, *You've gotta be kidding me! I'll never make it up that gigantic hill,* but I continued walking toward it. The closer I got to the hill, the bigger it got. *Am I really going to do this?* I reached the gravel road and started running. I was less than halfway up and started thinking there was no way I could make it to the top. I tried to visualize Jesus running with me. Finally, I told Him He was going to have to do it for me because my legs were going numb. I leaned on my brother, Jesus, and made it to the top. What a feeling of accomplishment!

On the way back to the cabin, I thought about how often I quit when things get hard. There have been so many times in my life when I have wanted to give up because something was hard. God has never failed to get me through each time. I was on my third attempt at finishing my dissertation when I finally wised up and quit trying to do it on my own. The third time was the charm for me because it took that long for me to invite God into the process. Apparently it was a lesson I didn't fully understand the first few times God tried to teach it to me. I asked myself, *Why do I keep trying to do things on my own? What am I not understanding?* I once heard someone say that God tests us to teach us, and if we don't pass the test the first time, we get to take it again. I had taken this one a few times until I finally got it.

On another walk/run, in the early spring, it was very wet and muddy outside. I usually go into the woods near my house, where the trails are very sandy. In some places, it is like being on a beach, but this time, it was muddy, and that made it all that much harder to run. Nevertheless, again God clearly spoke to me that He wanted me to run all the way out of the woods to end my three-mile loop. Of course it is uphill at the end, but not nearly as big as the other one. At this point, I was really frustrated with my weight. It had been almost a year since the diagnosis of low thyroid, and I was still struggling to get twelve pounds off. I felt defeated, but I didn't want to give up. Before the thyroid problem, I'd lost over forty pounds but had lived in fear of gaining it all back. I began to doubt that the running would do any good, so I finally asked God if the weight was ever going to come off. What I heard was sketchy. It was a yes, but I would have to suffer as Christ suffered. My first thought was, *Do I really have to suffer that much?* I finished the run by leaning on my brother and left the woods somewhat confused.

A couple days later, I experienced yet another aha moment in my life. I'd been thinking a lot about how much Christ suffered for us. His suffering is too much for my mind to wrap itself around, and it breaks my heart. As I pondered this, the light bulb went on. Christ came to bring us to the Father, and He did everything with the Father. He didn't have trust issues. He never tried to live outside the Father's will. He never went without listening to or hearing His Father's voice. He never lived without God. When He suffered, He drew strength and peace from the Father. First Peter 2:21,23 says:

> To this you were called, because Christ suffered for you, leaving you an example, that you should follow in his steps. When they hurled their insults at him, he did not retaliate; when he suffered, he made no threats. Instead, he entrusted himself to him who judges justly.

This may be elementary to others, but it was new to me. Maybe I was just ready to learn it. Many times, I'd tried to give this whole weight thing to God. What I really wanted was for Him to fix it for me, but what He wants is for me to lean on Him so He can show me how to do things for myself. Christ gave us the example to follow. When it is unbearable, when it really hurts, when we want to give up, when we are suffering, we are to press in even closer to the Father. I don't have to do that alone either because the sufferings become easier to bear with Him. This doesn't mean it won't hurt or that it will be easy. Christ was fully human and felt the pain, but He also knew where to find the peace that surpasses understanding.

There is new strength when I don't think I have any left. I need to lean on Him from the start and not wait until I have exhausted myself trying to do it on my own. I guess I am learning obedience from what I suffer (Hebrews 5:8), and that suffering as Christ suffered actually means God takes my burdens. As hard as it is to give up my own will, life really is easier when I do. What joy fills my heart to know that I don't walk this life alone!

Choices

I am often asked and even wonder myself, *Am I doing what God wants me to do?* I really love it when God is crystal clear in what He wants me to do, but that doesn't happen as often as I'd like. I've finally come to understand that our choices are not always simple this-or-that decisions with God. I've always thought there would be only two choices, a clear-cut, black-and-white decision between something that honors God and something that doesn't. It was up to me to figure out which was which.

Then, I had an aha moment that reminded me that God loves to include us in creating, and He knows we find joy in it. We are not robots. We are in relationship with Him, and relationships are about give and take. If we get to create with Him, why would He only give us one choice? I really believe He often lays out a variety of acceptable, honorable choices, then gives us the opportunity to choose the one that brings us the most joy.

My husband and I recently decided to buy a cabin for our family to enjoy. God was clear that it was something He wanted for us, but we had many choices as to which one we should purchase. I struggled with finding the right one. I thought I had rather clearly heard from God that we should buy an empty lot and build, and when we visited the lot, I really liked the location and the feel of the space. I told Curt I thought we should buy it.

Before we made that our final decision, however, we went

to another site we'd heard about, one with a ready-to-move-in cabin, well within our price range. We'd assumed we'd have to do a major remodel to anything we bought, as everything we'd looked at to that point was going to require a ton of work, possibly even tearing down and starting over. This cabin, though, felt like a place where we could relax, and we could afford it. My husband was ready to make an offer, but he questioned if I thought I was dishonoring God by not buying the lot.

I did have to spend some time with God to be sure of our decision, as I was worried at first that I was letting God down. I didn't want to go against Curt, as he was sold on it being the right place for us. Finally, God made it clear to me that we had more than one option that would still honor Him. We chose the one that said we could relax there. God lets us participate in decisions because He is a God who loves and values relationship. He loves working with us. He wants to give us our heart's desire, and we want to fulfill His.

I spent years simply asking God what I should do, expecting a simple, singular answer. After all, I was His servant, ready to do what was ordered. I am so grateful that He has shown me that I am His daughter, that he has revealed and shared the joy of creating and making choices.

In Genesis, God invites us to participate in creation, and this includes our lives. God gave us more than one choice in buying the cabin. The cabin was about finding a place of rest, but we chose which cabin we wanted. We experienced the joy of choosing our place to relax. God laid out a variety of choices for us, and all were pleasing to Him; we got to choose what was pleasing to us, and in that, we co-created our resting place. When He told me I could relax at whatever cabin we wanted, it was His way of saying, "This is a good choice too."

This is not to say there are not times when God asks us to do something specific, and in those instances, we must choose obedience. He may ask us to pray for someone or help someone in need, and it is all about submitting out of our relationship with Him. The opposite is also true: The enemy also can lure us with choices that go against love and grace. Discernment can be tricky, but love is a good barometer for each decision. If we have doubts about a decision, it is good to seek counsel from others, as long as we don't miss out on the joy of choice.

I have learned not to be burdened with the right choice but to follow my heart. If the choice is about love and joy, I know I am in line with God's will. I always seek God's guidance in decisions and do my best to follow His will. I have also learned to enjoy the process of creating with Him as I live in relationship with Him. I must say that it's more fun to have this kind of relationship than it would be to be a robot.

I hope cleaning house has been and will continue to be a blessing for you, as it is for me. As we continue to clean, it's my prayer that we continue to share our stories with others, for this is our directive. Paul says it best in 1 Corinthians 2:6-10:

> *We, of course, have plenty of wisdom to pass on to you once you get your feet on firm spiritual ground, but it's not popular wisdom, the fashionable wisdom of high-priced experts that will be out of date in a year or so. God's wisdom is something mysterious that goes deep into the interior of His purposes. You don't find it lying around on*

the surface. It's not the latest message, but more like the oldest—what God determined as the way to bring out His best in us, long before we ever arrived on the scene. The experts of our day haven't a clue about what this eternal plan is (MSG)

Paul says it is our responsibility to share our wisdom with others. We must share our stories with others to encourage them in their relationship with God and others. We also know it's not a magic plan. The housecleaning really only occurs through the Spirit. We have to be willing to let the Spirit dig deep. Paul continues to show us in 1 Corinthians 2:10-13:

The Spirit, not content to flit around on the surface, dives into the depths of God, and brings out what God planned all along. Who ever knows what you're thinking and planning except you yourself? The same with God—except that He not only knows what He's thinking, but He lets us in on it. God offers a full report on the gifts of life and salvation that He is giving us. We don't have to rely on the world's guesses and opinions. We didn't learn this by reading books or going to school; we learned it from God, who taught us person-to-person through Jesus, and we're passing it on to you in the same firsthand, personal way (MSG).

The beauty of my housecleaning has been that it's directed by God. God is the reason I've found new depths to love and joy in my life.

When I started this journey, I had no idea of the depths God would dig to bring me freedom. He will go to great lengths to bring each of us to a place of wholeness. He caused me to reevaluate my past and shined a new light in dark places. Cleaning behind the fridge isn't as scary as it once was. I can see the rewards He brings when I do the hard work of cleaning.

He taught me the power of forgiveness and the importance of doing the little things as we dust the furniture. What true power we have through Him! I learned to take seriously the authority I have when I vacuum. Lastly, I learned the value of staying grounded in Him daily through doing dishes. All of these lessons have given me a new approach to life and a renewed relationship with Him. I know if He will do it for me, He will do it for each one of us.

May we continually clean our houses, transform our minds, and rest solely in the One who loves deeply and completely!

Bibliography

Allender Ph.D., Dan B. (2008). *Wounded Heart: Hope For Victims of Childhood Sexual Abuse.* Colorado Springs, CO: NavPress.

Anderson, Neil T. & Park Dave. (1993). *The Bondage Breaker.* Eugene, OR: Harvest House Publisher.

Baker, John. (2007). *Life's Healing Choices.* West Monroe LA: Howard books.

Bell, Rob. (2007). *Sex God: Exploring The Endless Connections Between Sexuality and Spirituality.* Grand Rapids, MI: Zondervan.

Colbert M.D., Don. (2003). *Deadly Emotions: Understanding The Mind-Body-Spirit Connection That Can Heal or Destroy You.* Nashville, TN: Thomas Nelson.

Covey, Stephen. (1989). *7 Habits Of Highly Effective People.* New York: Free Press.

Foster, Richard J. (1988). *Celebration of Discipline.* New York: HarperCollins.

Frangipane, Francis. (2006). *The Three Battlegrounds: An In-Depth View of the Three Arenas of Spiritual Warfare: The Mind, the Church and the Heavenly Places.* Cedar Rapids, IA: Arrow Publications.

Frost, Jack (2002). *Experiencing The Father's Embrace.* Shippensburg, PA: Destiny Image.

Frost, Jack. (2006). *Spiritual Slavery to Spiritual Sonship: Your Destiny Awaits You.* Shippensburg, PA: Destiny Image.

Gardner, Thom. (2005). *Healing the Wounded Heart: Removing Obstacles To Intimacy With God.* Shippensburg, PA: Destiny Image.

Goll, James & Goll Michal Ann. (2006). *Dream Language: The Prophetic Of Dreams, Revelations And The Spirit Of Wisdom.* Shippensburg, PA: Destiny Image.

Hansel, Tim. (1987). *Holy Sweat.* Dallas: Word Publishing.

Hession, Roy. (1950). *The Calvary Road*. Fort Washington, PA: CLC Publications.

Jacobsen, Wayne. (2007). *He Loves Me! Learning to Live in the Father's Affection*. Newbury Park, CA: Windblown Media.

Maltz, Wendy. (2001). *The Sexual Healing Journey: A Guide for Survivors of Sexual Abuse (Revised Edition)*. Harper Perennial.

Milligan, Ira. (2000). *Understanding the Dreams You Dream Volume II*. Shippensburg, PA: Destiny Image.

Murray, Andrew. (2008). *Humility*. Radford, VA: Wilder Publications.

Nouwen, Henri J. M. (1972). *The Wounded Healer*. New York: Image Doubleday.

Ripka, Chuck. (2007). *God Out Of The Box: How Divine Interpretation Changed A Midwestern Town How Miracles Happen in the Marketplace How You Can Change Your World*. Lake Mary, FL: Charisma House.

Schroeder, Gerald L. (1997) *The Science Of God: The Convergence of Scientific and Biblical Wisdom*. New York: Free Press a division of Simon and Schuster.

Sheets, Dutch. (2007). *Authority in Prayer: Praying With Power And Purpose*. Grand Rapids, MI: Bethany House Publishers.

Virkler, Mark & Virkler Patti. (2002). Cheektowaga, NY: Lamad Publishing.

Willard, Dallas. (1999). *Hearing God: Developing A Conversational Relationship With God*. Downers Grove, IL: InterVarsity Press.

Winter, Jack & Ferris, Pamela. (1997). *The Home Coming: Unconditional Love, Finding Your Place In The Father's Heart*. Seattle, WA: YWAM Publishing.

Young, Wm. Paul. (2007). *The Shack*. Newbury Park, CA: Windblown Media.

Curriculum/DVD

Bell, Rob. (2007). *Everything is Spiritual.* USA: Zondervan.

Frost, Jack. (no date given). *Breaking Free: Uprooting Destructive Habits and Thought Patterns.* Shiloh Place Ministries: shilohplace.org.

May, Eddie. (2004). *The Turning: 12 Week Curriculum of Healing the Wounded Heart.* Agape Christian Family Center: agapepage.com.

Toyne, Kris (no date given). *Forgive and Forget???* Agape Christian Family Center: agapepage.com. (Message series).

Songs

Crowder, David. (2006). "No One Like You." *Illuminate.* Six Step Records.

Grant, Natalie. (2005). "Held." *Awaken.* Curb Records.

Smith, Jami. (2000) "Worship You." *WOW Worship: Orange.* Sony Records.

Smith, Michael W. (2004). "Healing Rain." *Healing Rain.* Reunion Records.

Websites

Jochmann, Carmen. (2009). *The Benefits Of Human Touch.* http://carmen-jochmann.suite101.com/the-benefits-of-human-touch-a155979.

Metanoia Ministries. http://metanoiaministries.org/

Plumbline Ministries. http://plumblineonline.com/Home_Page.php

Satir, Virginia. http://www.brainyquote.com/quotes/keywords/hugs.html.

Shiloh Place Ministries. http://www.shilohplace.org/

Sicheneder, Richard. Spirit of Truth and Freedom Ministries. http://www.thespiritoftruthandfreedom.com

About the Author

DR. MARY SCHULZE MICHENER earned her doctorate in education from the University of Minnesota and has more than 20 years of experience in youth and education ministry in the local church. She is currently teaching women how to receive help from Jesus, allowing Him to heal the dark places in their hearts, by facilitating group experiences and speaking through Best Life Ministries. Mary also provides encouragement through her blog at http://marymichener.com

She also works at Bethel University where she evaluates everything and advises doctoral students through the dissertation process. Mary, her husband, and two boys reside in Big Lake, Minnesota.

Connect with Mary
on her website: http://marymichener.com,
on Twitter @marysmichener,
or on her Facebook author page: Mary Schulze Michener.